The Right Road to Radical Freedom

Tibor R. Machan

SOCIETAS
essays in political
& cultural criticism

imprint-academic.com

Published in the UK by Societas
Imprint Academic, PO Box 200, Exeter EX5 5YX, UK

Published in the USA by Societas
Imprint Academic, Philosophy Documentation Center
PO Box 7147, Charlottesville, VA 22906-7147, USA

ISBN 9781845400187

A CIP catalogue record for this book is available from the
British Library and US Library of Congress

For Judy & Dave Threshie

Acknowledgments

I wish to thank the editors of the *Journal of Private Enterprise, The Journal of Ayn Rand Studies, The Personalist*, The Hoover Institution Press, and M&M Scrivener Press for permission to use materials in this book they have previously published. I want also to express my gratitude to Dick Wallace or Freedom Communications, Inc., the Pacific Research Institute and Chapman University for their support of my work on this and other projects.

Contents

Whether it comes from a despotic sovereign or an elected presi-
dent, from a murderous general or a beloved leader, I see power
as an inhuman and hateful phenomenon. ... I have always
looked on disobedience toward the oppressive as the only way to
use the miracle of having been born.

Oriana Fallaci
quoted in Margaret Talbot, "The Agitator,"
The New Yorker (June 5, 2006), p. 59

Why We Need Philosophy

In what sense is philosophy relevant to *everyone's* life?

Although most people have probably not considered how philosophy can or does touch their lives, some simple examples may show this connection. When, in anger perhaps, someone *blames the world* for his misfortunes, he implies a *basic belief*—even if he later might wish to modify or abandon it. When someone declares his love of life, in some joyous moment, he, too, is expressing a view of the world in general. Such explicit statements as "Everything is relative", "Words mean whatever one wishes them to mean", "None of us can help what we are", "Human existence is without meaning or purpose", and "Whatever the majority chooses is what should be done" all indicate very broad beliefs—ideas not just about one or two instances of a person's life or of what he witnesses.

It is sometimes argued, however, that ideas are mere epiphenomenona, or even simply follow actions—William James thought this as do some contemporary neuro-physiologists. But this can be explained by reference to the fact that ideas develop and are not some kind of static object, they are themselves a kind of action and when they occur in a logical sequence, their impact may actually be ahead of them, in a sense, since the logic of the idea is already giving guidance to action. In any case, ideas undoubtedly matter, because even the idea that they do not is an idea with potentially important consequences.

Not Just Gabbing

Philosophy is something quite specific: it is a human activity of a certain kind, not just any variety of gabbing, speculating, or debating.

In spite of the many differences among various philosophies, the field itself is specifiable. *Philosophy has as its purpose the identification and study of the most basic facts of reality and our relationship to them.*

From this abstract statement of what philosophy is we can now move on to fill in some of the details. First of all it will help to give an example of what some philosophers have considered a basic fact, and to suggest how human beings might relate to such a fact in their lives. Basic facts are rarely thought of in our everyday, normal experiences, since they are very obvious — just as on earth we rarely think about gravity, since it affects us always.

To characterize such facts, let us contrast them with the more ordinary kind. We often make note of such facts as that the moon is difficult to see in the daytime because the sun is bright, or that it is raining very hard in the Midwest. Such facts are of limited scope. Although they are simple enough to make evident, many other facts are required before these sorts can be understood and appreciated. In the first case, for example, the facts of the moon's, the sun's, and the daytime's existence are presupposed. Many such facts are encountered each moment, every day, and throughout a lifetime. But these are not basic facts, since they depend on too many other facts.

Specific Facts versus General Facts

A basic or fundamental fact would be something different. It would have very broad scope and would be evident on a very wide scale. For example, let us assume that it is a fact that everything that exists must be composed of material substance, that it must have mass, dimension, and weight. If what we are now assuming were correct, then anything that could exist would be composed of matter. Such a fact, if it were a fact, would have the entire universe as its scope, and all other facts we might encounter would have to include it as a feature, as a "background" fact.

We, in turn, would relate to existence, to all of reality, in a way that would be directly influenced by this basic fact. Thus, when discussing whether something or other exists or could exist, the answer we would give would depend first of all on whether the proposed item is composed of matter. Suppose now that it is shown that what is proposed to exist is not composed of matter. Then if it were true that everything that exists is composed of matter, we could conclude that the proposed thing simply does not and could not exist. So the assumed basic fact that everything is material relates to human life as a sort of basic guide to what we should accept as possible. If materialism is true, then it is impossible for something to exist that is not composed of matter: therefore, we should not bother with any suggestions to the contrary (except as a curiosity, perhaps).

This is just one illustration of what basic facts might be, and of what sort of inquiries philosophers might conduct.

Why We Need Philosophy

Is there an important role for philosophy in human life?

One aspect of philosophy evident in the ordinary philosophical remarks cited earlier, as well as in all major philosophical systems and schools, indicates the answer to our question. We can already detect the indispensability of philosophy to human life. Recall that all of the statements listed at the beginning of this discussion are very broad in their scope. They cover or refer to many things, many individual events, relationships, actions, institutions, or elements of whatever subject matter they involve. When a person says, "Life is nothing but struggle", the meaning of that statement includes all of life, from birth to death, without exception. "Words mean whatever one wishes them to mean" refers again to all words—even those used to make the statement. "You made your bed so you must lie in it" refers, metaphorically in this case, to all instances when a person chooses some course of action and is faced with the results.

If someone takes these thoughts seriously, and many do, it is very likely that such an individual's life will reflect what is meant by them. A person will most likely have an attitude toward, an anticipation of, or a regard for life that conforms to the belief expressed—or to the same belief held in silence. To see the impact of philosophical ideas we need to consider what will happen when a person takes such ideas seriously and lives by them.

Pervasive Impact

It is most likely that those who take such ideas seriously will find their impact evident throughout their lives. This can be so whether the ideas are worked out in great detail or held as firm conclusions without close scrutiny. Even in what might be considered less reflective, less systematically intellectual cultures, there is clear evidence that ideas such as those we have cited have considerable impact—in the form of myths, sayings, religious writings, and the like.

It should also be stressed that virtually everyone has some such general ideas. Whether explicitly stated, self-consciously believed, or merely accepted by habit, such ideas influence one's life. They sometimes govern entire cultures, even epochs of human history, as is evident today with Marxism throughout a considerable portion of the globe. In the last analysis, for philosophical purposes, the crucial issue is whether these ideas are correct. But their importance cannot be overstated.

We can go through life without ever becoming involved with horticulture, astronomy, or international relations, since these apply only within a limited range and only intermittently (though, of course, widely and often enough when compared with some other concerns). But philosophical ideas, by their nature, apply directly or indirectly to the basic features of existence and human life. For example, the philosophical idea that none of us can help what will happen in our lives pertains to all of everyone's life! That surely is not a restricted scope, and if the claim is true, it can have considerable bearing on how we should understand ourselves and others — whether, for instance, we can ever meaningfully hold others responsible for criminal activity, credit ourselves or others with achievements, and so forth.

Philosophical Nutrition

As the most general field of inquiry, philosophical concerns reflect on everything people think about and do.

Obviously one can live without explicit philosophical knowledge or convictions. One can also live without strict attention to one's health. Even without crucial nutrients a person can survive for quite some time. Many of the biological, chemical, psychological, and other requirements of life can be neglected without drastic immediate consequences. Therefore, if the issue is whether one *can* continue life without philosophy or some of its better contributions, then clearly the answer is yes. But this is not the issue, for one can live without many things that one *should* secure if they are even remotely possible.

Philosophy touches upon virtually every aspect of life — directly, when someone consciously, knowingly decides to invoke philosophical ideas, and indirectly, when a person absorbs such ideas on hearsay or must deal with others who have done so. Since philosophy focuses on the most basic principles of existence, and on our (proper) relationship to them, its results are of importance to anyone who wants to live successfully.

Chapter I

Free Will Reconsidered

Every discussion needs a starting point and this one is no different. Since this work focuses on the topic of freedom, I need to consider whether we are free to think and do as we choose or is our conduct being moved by forces apart from ourselves. This is the old issue of free will or human causal agency or initiative—there are different terms by which those who address it like to name the topic but it is basically the same thing. Do we as individual human beings choose our conduct, at least partly independently, freely?

In a review of my book, *Initiative: Human Agency and Society* (2000) William Dwyer (2001)assumes that compatibilism is coherent and so he concludes it is a superior account of human conscious life, including morality and the enormous diversity of it all, to that which I offer. Compatibilism can be understood in a variety of ways and Dwyer's is the most prominent among them. It suggests that although we are moved by forces that impinge on us and we do not initiate anything we do, not in the "independent" sense, this situation is compatible with moral responsibility. And that is that we are also bound to do certain things in life and avoid doing other things and can be held accountable for either, get praised for the former and blamed for the latter. The idea is that this moral responsibility is compatible with determinism.

There is a less well known yet I'd say more plausible version of compatibilism which holds that yes, we are determined to do what we do but it is we ourselves who do the determining. As when we say, "He was determined to win that woman's heart, no matter what." But this isn't the kind of compatibilism that Dwyer and many others are championing.

If the kind of compatibilism Dwyer, Daniel Dennett (1984) and others advocate were coherent, if it could make sense of morality and diversity as well as retain its form of determinism, the view would be very interesting and challenging. Alas, in fact compatibilism is simply hard determinism with some soft edges but as such it is not coherent—it eats its cake but still wants to have it, too. In light of this, the agent-causation based thesis of human initiative (or freedom of the human will) I have been defending is superior and thus more worthy of being believed than the alternatives to it. Let me elaborate.

At the very start Dwyer tells us that he thinks "that if I chose to be awake to the issues I am now facing, then I must have done so for a reason, which means that the reason determined my choice." Well I do not share this thought, for—not because of—two reasons.

First, making a choice in the sense in which I identify that act— namely, to take the initiative to apply one's mind to figuring things out in the world—does not require some given, prior reason for me to have done this, not in any specific sense other than that that is the kind of being I am, one that relates to the world via thinking about it and acting in line with the results. This is what I consider a *first* choice, one that can be made repeatedly—as when one keeps in focus, pays close attention to the world, is continuously awake to it—but it is so fundamental that no prior knowledge is required for it. And there is good precedent for thinking that no such prior knowledge is required for making such a choice—criminal law, in general, assumes that ignorance is no excuse. This means that some matters we ought to come to know and if we have not, that is our fault and we can be held responsible for the negligence involved in not having come to know what we should have come to know. This is evident also in ordinary life, apart from the law, when folks who have failed to consider something blamed themselves by saying, "Damn it, I didn't think," without then saying, "Because I believed that not thinking would be justified."

Second, a reason is not anything like a cause, some variable or factor that moves something to end up in a certain state. This is because a reason is a conviction or idea formed by the agent who might not have formed it. So it is the agent who forms a reason for which he or she might take an action.

I *may* reflect on some issue and form an idea which then I *may* use to derive some additional idea, including the idea of doing something I *may* then go ahead and do. At each turn I am free to suspend the thinking process, although I may well cultivate my character so that this is less and less likely. So the reason didn't make me do anything, I did.

To identify reasons with causes is to beg a question that has been at issue in the discussion of free will. As I suggest above, however, it is most reasonable to hold that a reason is not a cause — it is sui generis, the grounding of my action in a human being's mind, as it were, not something that is replicated elsewhere in the world as causes are.[1]

Let me focus now on Dwyer's frequent use of a particular locution. He tells us several times that what I explain or give an account of in terms of the free choices people make could "easily be explained" by reference to various causes. I doubt this, very seriously. His claim to this effect is at best question begging and assumes that his own preferred compatibilism has already been shown to be right.

Indeed, Dwyer gives no general reason to think that what is explainable by reference to initiative can be given an (event-) causal explanation. Instead, he offers a mere promissory note, as do most determinists who say that what hasn't yet been explained by reference to various causes will, in time, be so explained — say, the variations of Bach's compositions or the individuality of nearly all major painters. In the position I consider correct there is indexed much that render these phenomena and millions of similar ones explainable (in the sense of giving a coherent, rational account of them).

I want to reiterate the point, also, that objective knowledge is unexplained by reference to non-agent causes because then its important ingredient of being independent of preconceptions or prejudices would be missing. If my conclusion about O. J. Simpson's guilt is caused by X — some factor other than *my own initiated reflection on the evidence and arguments* regarding the issue — then this conclusion is something I did not reach independently and it must be what we would normally deem arbitrary, indeed, not *my* own conclusion at all.

Let me now turn to Dwyer's preferred alternative, soft determinism, which is the one championed by Dennett. Given the way compatibilists and Dwyer conceive of this doctrine — namely, that as it understands the conscious world, it would be possible to have both a causal explanation of human conduct as well as its being the

[1] It is my position that the perplexing nature of the free will issue, as well as those of the nature of meaning, intention, conceptual consciousness and others like these, has a lot to do with the fact that these are unique feature of the world, emerging with human life, mainly, so it is very difficult to compare them with other phenomena that we know throughout nature. (This is perhaps one of the main reasons it is so tempting for many — for example Plato, Descartes, and Kant) to introduce notions dependent upon the supernatural when this topic arises.)

agent's responsibility to have engaged in that conduct – of course the theory succeeds better than all others, including the one I find most convincing. Such a view would manage a combination that is by all counts impossible – one's being the agent of one's conduct, as well as one's being a mere link in a chain of causation leading, unavoidably, to the behavior that under a different understanding is construed as one's conduct.[2]

But it is misguided to think that such a doctrine could be right – no *bona fide*, ultimate personal responsibility can be attached to behavior that is, let's say, softly determined. And Dennett & Co. do admit that the will isn't free from the impact of various forces that ultimate make it do what it does (which in my terms means that a person, whose will is but a theoretical starting point of action, isn't free as he or she acts other than in the sense that *no other person* is doing what he or she does). This isn't a defense of any kind of free action at all and thus not of any kind of moral responsibility which credits the agent as the source of right or wrong conduct. Absent the possibility of so crediting a person, the idea of moral credit or blame is a *non-sequitur*.

A better idea of soft determinism is just what its major proponents, such as Hume, had in mind. This is that instead of some fact(s) or event(s) causing one's behavior, some fact(s) or event(s) causes the human will to acquire certain attributes which, then, cause one's behavior. This might be envisioned along lines of a hammer that does not directly strike a nail but, instead, strikes a piece of rubber that is placed between it and the nail (say, when one wishes to protect the precious metal of which the nail is made). The nail moves, however, because of the hammer's striking of the rubber which then pushes the nail. The will that Hume and others position between the cause and the behavior takes the place of the piece of rubber. And clearly this does not introduce any kind of independent agency for the nail, despite its being a step removed from the hammer in consequence of it.

Similarly, if the human will has been shaped by prior facts or events that cause one's behavior, then such a will provides no – indeed, prevents any – independent agency to account for one's behavior. In short, one's actions then aren't free but deter-

---

[2]   Dennett actually tries to argue that we have evolved to be able to engage in avoidance, so our behavior doesn't come about unavoidably since we are often able to avoid some actions. Yet, this means only that we have been caused by various factors to behave in a way that is different from what had been anticipated.

mined. This is indeed what some defense attorneys like to argue to exonerate their clients seeing that being determined in this way renders personal responsibility for the commission of a crime quite impossible. Now, if soft determinism is seen as every bit the determinism that hard determinism is, it is no longer plausible to see it combining the crucial aspects of the sort of determinism that excludes free will — namely, efficient causal explanation of behavior — and moral responsibility — namely, the agent's own independence rendering him or her the cause of his or her ensuing conduct.

The only compatibilist view that makes sense is one whereby the human being is the determining agent — or cause, if you will — in accounting for that human being's conduct. In that sense I am a determinist, along the lines of Roger W. Sperry and some other agent causation theorists of free will.[3] The nature of the being we are, its being a volitionally conscious entity, does determine — in the neo-Aristotelian fashion Dwyer mentions but for opposite purposes — what it can do. But in the case of each human individual, it is that individual who will determine what it will do.

Several minor points need now be touched upon so as to complete this brief response.

Someone's interest in something is not a sufficient cause for doing anything — one may well choose to resist this interest (as, indeed, most responsible people do with many of their fleeting or even persistent interests). This same goes, also, for desires and other so called motives. (The language of motivation is highly influenced by deterministic analysis since it arose out of the attempt to reconcile accounts of human conduct with accounts of the behavior of physical objects, as in Hobbes.)

A choice of the sort that is at issue in the free will vs. determinism dispute needs to be distinguished from a choice that is at issue in selecting one item or course from many alternatives. In the latter case knowledge of the various alternatives is already required, in the former there are only two alternatives and no prior knowledge is required in order to end up with one or the other. That is why such a choice is basic, a matter of initiative or creation. (It is precisely because no such prior knowledge exists that in Ayn Rand's and my view the failure to make that choice constitutes opting out of the moral game and, indeed, life itself! Once the choice to think is made, then it follows that one has signed up for life, as it were, and this is

---

[3] See, among others, Timothy O'Connor (2000), David Deutsch (1997), pp. 338–39 and James Robert Brown (1994), p. 64.

why it would be immoral to evade thinking henceforth — it would be a sort of breach of an oath.)[4]

Animals may exhibit a kind of self-determination but because of their type of consciousness this self that is performing the determination is understood to be the result, without remainder, of the interaction of their biological make-up and perceptions of the constituents of their environment. (It is interesting that Mr. Dwyer does not note in his discussion of this point something he acknowledges at another, namely, that the mere possibility of self-determination does not establish that something is actually determining its own conduct.)

There is much else that could be discussed but I have tried to do most of it in my book and hope those interested in the debate will consult what I wrote there, not just a review of it.[5] I want to conclude by simply noting that while Ayn Rand has inspired much of my thinking in these and other matters, Rand's and her students' work must be treated independently of mine. There are innumerable nuances in this discussion and some of us have dealt with them differently from how others did and this can make the difference as to which is the better account of the free will position, let alone of how to understand human conduct.

---

[4]   For more, see Machan (2006).
[5]   For a very thorough and fascinating collection of essays on this topic, see Libet et al. (1999). In my view it is Libet who comes closest to the right solution to the problems involved, in his contribution to that volume, "Do We Have Free Will?" (There is an aspect of Libet's view that is, I believe, misguided: His belief that all conscious action is preceded by some unconscious intention. What I believe Libet's research has found is that all self-conscious or deliberate action is preceded by conscious intention of which we aren't yet aware. There is a lot of that going on, of course — most conscious action does not become self-conscious.)

Chapter II
Politics, Faith and God's Non-Existence

Introduction: Politics & Pluralism

Embracing a political system in pluralistic societies via a specific faith, be it Christian, Muslim, Hindu or whatever, runs into trouble when we consider that a political order, in principle, requires understanding from all those comprising the body politic. In a multi-religious, multi-cultural society such as the USA, Canada, Australia, New Zealand, France, and so forth, one faith is clearly inadequate to provide such publicly accessible justification for the political principles by which the society is to be governed. Yet there are influential public intellectuals, such as Richard John Neuhaus, in his several works, especially *Time Toward Home* (1975), who champion just such a theocratic alternative to the relatively secular American and other Western polities.

In an absolute monarchy the monarch alone would establish the country's laws and if he is of one faith or another, that is where the justification for the laws could come from. Something similar would occur in religiously homogenous countries since the population would be of one faith and even though that faith might rest on quicksand, so long as it is barely challenged, it can function as the foundation of law and order.

But in a pluralistic society where everyone has the right to ask by what authority the law exists and the government governs, reliance on a faith peculiar to even a vast majority is not sufficient. A naturalistic justification is needed. This is why "creator" was—but "God" would not have been—a wise choice for the American founders as they crafted the Declaration of Independence.

God & Reason

Some will argue that the issue of God's existence can be resolved without resorting to specific faiths. They will advance various arguments, accessible to public scrutiny by nearly everyone (or at least all those not crucially incapacitated), in order to demonstrate that God exists and given His nature, something as vital as the issue of what kind of human community is fitting for us to live in cannot be divorced from Him. Their politics is in the Augustinian tradition, Thomist, or, especially, Spinozist, whereby the nature of goodness and justice are unavoidably tied to theological considerations that converge on the principles of Nature itself. A very contemporary variety of these sorts of arguments is dubbed "Intelligent Design."

Is there good reason to take that route to understanding human political life? Which is to ask, ultimately, does God exist?

The first point to take up is what the question asks. Does it mean: "Is God part of the world, do we have sound justification for believing that the claim is true?" Or does it mean "Is a Supernatural God real?" And if the latter, what criteria of reality is to be applied to searching out the answer for something that is supposed to be prior to or transcendent of reality?

Indeed, a problem in approaching the issue is that, as many believers maintain, God isn't supposed to be of this world — as would be, say, even such curious imagined beings as unicorns, mermaids, or UFOs — but logically prior to and/or transcendent, which is to say in some sense beyond it. That is to say, God is the sort of being we do not find among all the other beings in the world but is supposed to exist in some other sense or dimension or realm.

There are, of course, peculiar, esoteric conceptions of God, some of which would be subject to rational scrutiny — for example, Aristotle's unmoved mover. Yet it is highly questionable that any of the major religions of our time could accept such a minimalist — virtually Spinozist — conception of the deity. If anything, Aristotle, as well as Spinoza, advanced a *scientific* or metaphysical idea of how the world is to be understood and the term "God" was used merely to signify the special nature of the causal power of the beginning of it, nothing more. Such an extremely minimalist view of God is not at issue in the debates surrounding God's existence, including the nature of the supposed "creator" mentioned in the Declaration of Independence.

God's existence is, thus, supposed to be unique, unlike the existence of anything else in the world of which we can learn in familiar ways — e.g., going on an expedition, doing experiments, finding that it makes good sense of our experiences (e.g., a jealous motive), etc. As Anselm noted, even an atheist would admit that this is how we think of God, as such a unique, extraordinary being.

So what is the nature of God, what do we mean by "existence" for such an entity.

God's Nature in Theism

What we are usually asked to accept is that God is an omniscient, omnipotent, omni benevolent, and eternal being.

Thus not only have we no direct, ordinary experience of God, and are thus unable to infer God's existence from some well grounded and, therefore, sound theory; neither does God come to light upon analyzing some experiences and looking for something that underlies them. (There are exceptions to this: the Intelligent Design — a variety of the Cosmological — argument supposedly infers — or abducts — a grand designer, dubbed "God," from the orderliness of the universe.)[1]

It actually seems that none of these approaches could prove to us God's existence for that is not subject to being established in any mundane fashion.

What then is left? Some say that there is a familiar way to establishing God's existence, namely, by way of the argument from best explanation. As one believer puts it, "We accept hypotheses of all kinds based upon what we may loosely call their explanatory power. In this case the hypothesis is of a mysterious being, not in conformity with the ontology of others explanatory entities, yet in a certain respect like them: without its existence, even as a mysterious being, the world itself could not exist."[2]

In response to this it can be argued that it is difficult to see that God's existence provides an explanation for anything not explainable in less problematic — less grandiose, more familiar, not internally confusing terms. Although in many explanations — e.g., when

---

[1] C.S. Peirce's idea of abduction may be explained by the following general pattern of reasoning deployed in the argument for Intelligent Design: The surprising phenomenon, X, is observed (orderly phenomena that Darwinian evolutionary theory does not handle [yet]). Among hypotheses A, B, and C, A [a grand Intelligent Designer=God] is capable of explaining X. Hence, there is a reason to pursue (or believe in) A. See, for more, http://seamonkey.ed.asu.edu/~alex/pub/Peirce/Logic_of_EDA.html#l ogical.

[2] Personal e-mail communication from Mark Turiano.

we postulate the infinity of space so as to make sense of some phenomena in astrophysics — the thing posited "outstrips by a lot" what
is supposed to be explained by it, there is usually nothing internally
incoherent about it. But God is very problematic because His charac-
teristics seem not to be able to coexist. For example, omniscience and
omnipotence appear to conflict in certain respects, as do omnipotence and omni benevolence.

Turning, for a moment, to the recent consideration of the existence
of God, based on the argument that some of what we witness in the
world is unexplained by natural means and postulating and Intelligent Designer (=God) is the best explanation, here are the serious
problems with this. For one, the world isn't all that orderly, at least
by any ordinary standards — human life, especially, is filled with dis-
order, and much of the animate world can be so regarded, as well. A
tsunami, here, an massive earthquake there, a plague somewhere
else, AIDs, and so forth, all these do not testify to a supremely
orderly world.

A Randian Problem with ID

But assuming that all these are orderly in the sense that they obey the
laws of physics, biology, etc., is it credible to explain them by way of
the hypothesis of a grand Intelligent Designer? Here is where
Objectivism's famous "stolen concept fallacy" kicks in powerfully.

Intelligence itself is a function, power, or activity of a living brain
— *when one is intelligent, this is in part due to one's activation of mental
powers that are made possible from the biological organ of one's brain.* But a
brain is part of the world. To assume that before the world there
existed intelligence is to commit a fallacy dubbed "the stolen concept," assuming something can exist without its foundations.[3]

Another excellent example of the fallacy is on exhibit in the following quote: "Reason itself is a matter of faith. It is an act of faith to
assert that our thoughts have any relation to reality at all."[4] This ploy
is frequently utilized by apologists for faith. It reminds me of people
who excuse adultery by claiming that all marriage in reality is nothing but prostitution.

But one reply to all these logical points is that what is illogical or
conceptually confusing in matters of religious belief is merely additional evidence of God's innate mysteriousness, something we just

---

[3]   http://www.nathanielbranden.net/ess/ton04.html
[4]   G.K. Chesterton, quoted by Jon Meacham, *New York Times Book Review*,
Dec. 25, 2005 p. 10.

do not, indeed cannot, grasp (as fideism maintains). God's innate mysteriousness, at least to human inquirers, makes God a difficult to understand but by no means impossible explanation. Yet this will not help because the mere (logical) possibility of something being an explanation that hasn't been shown to be one doesn't establish that it is, in fact, such an explanation. It's no more than a fantasy, a Disney-like object of the imagination and surely serious believers would not find that acceptable as a case for God's existence.

God's nature as something defying nature that's studied in physics, chemistry, biology, etc., is the most serious problem for ID. How can something intend or design, without the brain that enables something to have thoughts and make judgments and formulate patterns? Or, how can God communicate without any of the facilities or faculties that make communication part of the world? How can God be a cause without any of the familiar attributes that enable things to produce other things?

More generally, and to reiterate, how can something explain the existence of something else if it is impossible to reconcile some of its own properties: e.g., omniscience, omnipotence and omni benevolence with the clear presence of bad things within the realm supposedly explained by God. At least the sort of God associated with major religions, such as Roman Catholicism, seems to invite puzzles rather than solve them. For example, God is supposed to make possible at least one virgin birth, the rising of some dead persons, the raising of the dead by some other persons, the changing of water into wine, the presence of three persons in one, and other miracles.

Moreover, God is by its very essence mysterious, supernatural, whereas explanations are within the province of the rational and natural — we explain the wet pavement (a natural phenomenon) by hypothesizing rain (another natural phenomenon) because rain is (most reasonably, based on experience) the highly probable cause of wet pavement. The orderliness of various microbiological phenomena that hasn't been fully satisfactorily explained by natural selection and other natural evolutionary processes isn't successfully explained by God, a mysterious, supernatural being that by its very nature can interact with whatever it would interact with in an infinite possible ways. That idea is not a hypothesis of an explanation but the invocation of a sort of Cole Porter type "anything goes" principle that has no place in a rational understanding of anything. An explanation, in other words, is good when it clears things up, not when it produces more puzzles than existed before its acceptance.

Indeed, the only problem a personal, intentional God's existence seems to promise to solve is the origin of the universe, although even here it immediately introduces a corresponding problem, namely, the existence of God ex nihilo. Indeed, if God could exist eternally, as the solution to this problem is often put, why could that same solution not be introduced for the existence of the universe? Why couldn't the universe have existed forever—after all, from nothing, nothing can come, nor can something turn into nothing. So, if the completely mysterious entity God could exist eternally, so might the much more comprehensible, if not of course fully understood, universe do so as well.

Some Thomist Issues

A Thomist might be tempted to argue here that an entity which eternally exists and does not change its nature, is a different kind of entity from the universe, which does. Yet there are some things that do not change for the universe either, such as its most basic (metaphysical) laws, the laws of being qua being (to which a Thomist will certainly attest). Whether we accept the Big Bang or plasma (steady state) theory, in either case there is no reason to hold that the universe began or will end, even if its composition or structure will. Beginnings and endings are a feature of what exists in the universe, not of the universe itself—it is the fallacy of composition to think otherwise.

So in this sense there is already something about the universe, its eternal being, that meets what we look for in explaining the universe —a point Spinoza notes in his recasting of theism in atheistic, i.e., non-theistic, terms.

It bears noting here that the likes of Neuhaus are intelligent enough to recommend not evangelical or scriptural fundamentalism as the source of political principles but Thomist natural law theory. Yet, insofar as the natural laws rest on divine will or ordination, they will also rest on quicksand and will not have a chance of convincing those not already among the faithful.

God May be a Pragmatic Option

Maybe, however, we ought to believe for pragmatic reasons, because it pleases us to do so? We certainly involve ourselves in numerous ventures that aren't based on truth—the whole fascination with games, sports, magic, art in general, etc., would appear to attest to this. So why not believe in God if it makes one feel good? Why not consider such a belief simply life-enriching?

First, those other non-truth related matters are pretty much optional and those few who have no affinity for them aren't supposed to be sinners, on their way to hell or missing out on something most important in life (unless one considers what is said by the football, soccer, or baseball fans of some North or Latin American or European city, or some university). Second, no one attributes truth value to claims about who ought to win or lose in sports, who ought to succeed or fail in the arts. It is all pretty optional, to be determined as a matter of talent and effort.

In religion, however, God is supposed to be real, one's belief in God obligatory, one's failure to believe devastating for one's eternal salvation, and others often authorized to coerce or at least cajole one to adhere if one is indifferent or does not see the point.

Is Necessary Existence Enough for God?

The last substantive point to consider is whether mere acceptance of the necessity of existence — of necessary being — may not suffice as the existence of God. This is what Charles Hartshorne believed.[5] But why should that suffice in the face of the overwhelming use of the term "God" for a being or beings that purportedly are far more than being necessarily existent. The principle of non-contradiction, for example, may be said to be necessarily existent — it is a principle that holds in any possible universe, to use a familiar way of putting it. But one would not confuse it with God, would one?

Still, as W. Somerset Maugham put the matter, "If the mystical experience is a liberating sense of community with what for want of a better word we name reality, and this you can call as you will the Absolute or God, then at some time we are all in greater or lesser degree mystics." (Somerset Maugham, 1970.)

Should Faith be Trusted?

So we turn to the next step in this inquiry, namely, when it is advanced that we need to believe in God's existence on the basis of faith. Faith is the sort of ground of belief that goes against and despite experience or argument. As Aquinas reportedly put it, "in faith the assent … is not caused by the thought but by the will." One has faith in someone one no longer can trust — as a wife may have

---

[5]   http://plato.stanford.edu/entries/hartshorne/

faith in a repeatedly philandering husband, despite all the evidence. It takes faith to believe that this man will never repeat his betrayals.

Granted, theists do not advise that we have faith about everything, not directly. Yet by implication they do advise that some important aspects of nearly everything ought to be taken on faith. The more radical of Christian Scientists ask us to abandon the help of physicians because we are essentially spiritual beings and prayer to God will be a much better road to healing ourselves and our children than relying on the work of medical doctors. Jehovah's Witnesses condemn blood transfusion as a matter of their faith despite the evident service the process affords in certain medical emergencies. And even religions without such drastic doctrines counsel that we should spend time on prayer, meditation, reading the Bible, etc., and forswear mundane ventures we could be embarking upon, as a matter of our underlying faith in God.

The question then is, "Is it right for us to believe in something (very important, widely influential in our lives) on the basis of faith?" Nothing supports this idea. We ought perhaps to believe, on faith, that our neighbors will treat us well, even if the evidence of such treatment among human beings is feeble, yet we are in need of the neighbor's kindness just now. Even this is more like hope or trust than faith, since some clear cases of trustworthiness back us up here. Maybe the case of having faith in the untrustworthy husband or wife is at least excusable.

But ought we to convict criminals on the basis of faith? We would be doing an injustice. Given the importance of the issue of whether someone ought to be incarcerated, we need to prove their guilt beyond a reasonable doubt, otherwise we need to remain unconvinced. Also, if we recommended medication or the doctor's treatment on the basis of no more than faith, we would face malpractice lawsuits. (We do often simply have faith that some psychological therapy will work, even when we have little or no evidence that it has helped anyone. This, too, seems more like hope than faith, since faith arises in the face of contrary evidence. Some theologians actually argue that the beauty of faith lies in its contradicting evidence, argument—otherwise it wouldn't merit rewards.)

Is it not evident that if we lead our lives on the basis of faith, we most probably would soon perish? It seems to be so—indeed, the young people on hallucinogenic drugs did have faith that they could fly when they jumped off buildings and so killed themselves. It is not enough to respond well, but faith in God is something limited, not all-embracing of the important issues in life. In most ordinary religions we are asked, point blank, to trust God in everything, to follow scripture or some organized religion's interpretation of it, because it is God's word. The faith of Abraham, who is told by God, the Bible says, "Take your son, your only son Isaac, whom you love, and go to the land of Moriah, and offer him there as a burnt offering on one of the mountains that I shall show you" (Gen. 22.2 NRSV) and complies shows greater integrity, at least, than the faith professed by those who somehow imagine they can delineate the things of faith and the things of reason. So faith, from the viewpoint of trying to prepare for living a successful human life, seems to be a luxury, to be indulged when serious matters of human living have been handled by doctors, engineers, attorneys or farmers.

But even if we did believe on the basis of faith, in this case what is it we are asked to believe in, apart from the myriad stories told by different religions via their good books and those who claim to know their meaning? At heart, we are asked to accept on faith the existence of an omniscient, omnipotent, eternal, omni-benevolent being.

Can such a being be understood to exist? Can, to go back to a child's innocent but telling question, God create an object so big that He cannot lift it? Why doesn't God eliminate bad things — diseases, earthquakes, tornadoes, viruses — that kill the innocent by the thousands? It would be vicious for an able human being to stand by while witnessing preventable disasters. (This is not the same as why He doesn't eliminate human evil, for which a somewhat plausible answer may be available.)[6] Furthermore, how would free choice be possible if God already knows everything? How could God cause the existence of the universe when causes are part of the universe?

---

[6]   It is argued by some that although God's powers and benevolence would not ordinarily make the existence of misery for the innocent, caused, especially, by natural catastrophes, impossible, here is where faith and God's mystery must be factored into the discussion. God must have something ultimately good in mind for those who so suffer!

      It seems to me that this simply stresses credibility. Say I sit on a sidewalk bench reading my paper and suddenly notice that a stroller with a baby has rolled on to the street and a big truck is headed right at it and I can just get up and hurry to it and rescue the baby. What justification could I possibly have for deliberately, not even just negligently, ignoring this and continuing with the reading of my paper? To believe that someone with the power to rescue the innocent and who is the best that anything could possibly be just does not carry out the rescue simply stretches the imagination so much that it cannot be fathomed.

Belief in God is not only unjustified but morally suspect. Even if God existed this would be true: indeed, that is the story of my change from Roman Catholic theism to atheism. I thought that even if there is a God who created us, we would be betraying ourselves and thus God, by believing in Him against all reason that we have been endowed with so as to guide our lives.

The issue of God's existence is, in the last analysis, the issue of whether we human beings ought to believe in God's existence. There is no way independent of this that God's existence can be considered. But, it seems, we violate the norms derivable from our understanding of human nature if we believe important things, including that God exists, on the basis of faith. So we ought not believe that God exists. This need not be some final judgment on the matter—we ought not believe a lot of things that could, in time, warrant belief. But we cannot be held responsible to hold beliefs we cannot sensibly form.

Principles of Human Community Life Can't Rest on Faiths

Yet, in a free society the fact that everyone is to reach conclusions freely, that no one may be forced to think even the right way, is so central that respect for it is essential. It is not another's belief that everyone is required to respect but the fact that it is that other who is to make the decision as to what he or she will believe.

However, presupposed in these last reflections is the naturalist, humanist—Lockean, Jeffersonian—conviction that everyone is free and independent by virtue of human nature. This idea transcends all the faiths and specific convictions about how we ought to live and therefore serves best as the general framework for organizing human community life. It is superior to any particular sectarian notion as to how society ought to be organized because it makes room for all peaceful alternative notions.

The importance of this conclusion is not something widely missed, in fact. I believe the American Founders chose to put their political creed so that it can be interpreted both in religious and secular terms precisely because they did not wish to tie the case of individual liberty and a regime that guards it to any given faith but wanted it to be understandable, at least in principle, by all who have political interests.

Summary and Conclusion

So, in conclusion let me summarize my points above: When we discuss political economy, resting our case on faith places it on wobbly foundations. By "faith" I mean a mode of believing based on acceptance or commitment, often despite systematic evidence to the contrary, or belief not based on supporting evidence of the sort available for systematic, organized, public scrutiny. Indeed, faith is often taken by its champions and adherents to be something extra rational. Its merit lies, supposedly, in the fact that it isn't based on evidence or reason but often contradicts both. Thus it is harder to sustain — and it is this difficulty that makes it a noble achievement to have and keep such a faith. If it were a conviction or belief based on evidence and reason it would lack this element, or so one hears it from some theologians and religious leaders.

But the problem with faith is that, especially concerning matters of public policy, but even vis-à-vis personal and social problems, it is rather hopeless to expect congruence or agreement to arise among very different people with different experiences, traditions, and religious convictions which are themselves based on faith. How, then, can faith be used to reach common or public convictions?[7]

Faith is a very private mental disposition. In many theological systems it is supposed to be at God's discretion whether someone will have faith or not. Augustine, for example, saw it as something that people acquired by the grace of God. Within this tradition, human beings are in a sense impotent when it comes to gaining faith — they are either graced with it or not.

But in matters of importance to many people — not to mention to all — it is futile to rely on such a method of reaching understanding and convictions. Indeed, there is a virtual guarantee of discord when faith is invoked. It may be appreciated, in this light, why there are nearly 4,200 different religions in the United States alone, why so many of the conflicts around the globe find much of their source in religious views, and why religion is something that many people refuse to debate or argue (since, again, one either has or doesn't have it).

To be sure, religion has been present for most of history. As George Orwell illustrates in his classic book and indictment of communism, Animal Farm, there is always a priest or minister around no matter what politics happen to dominate. Thus, Roman Catholic and other churches didn't even collapse under the self-proclaimed atheistic system of communism and managed to live peacefully within others. The presence of religion in nearly all epochs and societies, however, is no argument for the truth of much of what these

---

[7]   For a superb examination of the problem of faith in God, see Kenny (2004).

religions proclaim – after all, most societies hold widespread super-stitions, such as astrology, as well as all kinds of criminal institu-tions, which arguably rest on various false beliefs about how we all should live. The pervasiveness of these doesn't render them true. Nonetheless, it is probably because religions contain something of importance to human life, like codes of conduct that resonate so suf-ficiently with common sense, that they have staying power. And there is also the problem that secular philosophies haven't been suf-ficiently attentive to ethics or morality – often claiming that these, too, along with the descriptive parts of theologies, are myths. This isn't a credible view and religions have thrived by holding that they alone can provide people with ethics for guiding their lives.

There are also many heroic acts by religious people against vari-ous forms of tyranny. But these don't render the general outlook of the heroes true. For example, Roman Catholic Cardinal Mindszenty of Hungary opposed the Stalinist regime in his country, invoking grounds that any secular liberal thinker could appreciate. Lord Acton's liberalism isn't especially wedded to religion even though he himself was Catholic. Although the real concerns many religious people have about tyrannies and totalitarian regimes needn't be based on any specifically religious convictions – unless, of course, everything one believes rests on those – the ethical leadership provided from within religion has been significant in fighting such systems.

The bottom line is that what makes us human, most of all, is that we use reason and need to do so to make headway in our daily lives. In a country fit for human survival and for thriving, religion can't be a basis for public policy. That's why resting beliefs on the common capacity to reason, instead of on faith, and the need to discuss with others how one should lead one's life, has greater promise for peace and justice, especially in organized human communities inhabited by very different people.

So, one crucial reason that religiously based public policies have dubious merit is that their justification can't be examined along lines available to us in virtue of our humanity alone. A human commu-nity, as opposed to a sectarian or religious one, can't rest its institu-tions on what arises from faith – especially not if those institutions aim to be considered fairly and openly by all those who might be citi-zens, including members of very different religious denominations as well as many who lack any such membership.

Chapter III
Individualism

Individualism is central to Libertarianism, to the philosophy of a fully free society in the classical liberal tradition, including, to Objectivist politics.[1] Individuals are ends in themselves as understood in these positions and they may not be sacrificed to something else unless they deem that a goal they want to pursue.

I'll give you just one example of how sacrifice works in an individualist framework: Individually we each sometimes choose to undergo some pain or sacrifice for a greater benefit or to avoid a greater harm. We go to the dentist who hurts us so as to avoid worse suffering later; we do some unpleasant work for its beneficial results. Some persons take up an unpleasant, demanding diet so as to improve their health or looks, and some save money by foregoing benefits now so as to gain benefits when they are older. In each case, a cost is born by an individual for the sake of some benefit of his or her choosing.

So, why not similarly hold that some persons must, like it or not, bear some cost so as to benefit other persons or for the sake of the overall social good? The reason is that there just is no social entity the good of which can require someone's involuntary sacrifice. As the later Robert Nozick put it,

> There are only individual people — different individual people — with their own individual lives. Using one of these people for the benefit of others uses him and benefits the others. Nothing more. What happens is that something is done to him for the sake of others. Talk of an overall social good covers this up.

Nozick adds, parenthetically, "intentionally".

---

[1]   Objectivism is today the most comprehensive philosophical system in which the idea of a fully free society, with a legal order of minimal government, is defended. Other libertarian positions tend to leave open various philosophical issues and defend only the political thesis of minarchism (or anarchism). For more, see Long & Machan (2007).

To use a person in this way does not sufficiently respect and take account of the fact that he's a separate person — this is the only life he has. He does not get some over-balancing good from his sacrifice, and no one is entitled to force this upon him — least of all, a state or government that claims his allegiance as other individuals do not — and that therefore scrupulously must be neutral between its citizens. (Nozick [1974], pp. 32–33).

Now of course, Ayn Rand's devotion to individualism is widely known and need not be revisited here. Also, the concept of the individual person has a very significant role in classical liberalism, including neoclassical or Austrian economic analysis. In all of these contemporary libertarians testify to their link to individualism. So it's important to see whether this individualism has any good foundations or is it, as Marxists, neo-Marxists and communitarians claim, an invention, an ideology, one that may have served only certain purposes during a period of human history — for example, the acceleration of productivity by giving people the illusion that they are working for themselves and thereby spurring them on, providing them with incentives they otherwise would lack for the time being. (For Marx, the "new man" would no longer need such incentives.)

There are serious challenges to individualism, thus to classical liberalism, and to libertarianism even today. People such as Charles Taylor, the famous Canadian philosopher, write works to show that individualism is actually an implausible type of atomism. Atomism is supposed to be what individualism amounts to, the contention that we are isolated individuals — separate, independent, capable of sustaining ourselves without any linkage to others. This, according to the critics such as Taylor, Etzioni, Spragens, et al., is supposed to be a necessary but false, and thus fatal, philosophical ingredient of the Libertarian political outlook. Communitarianism in America is today lead by sociologist Amitai Etzioni who contends, along with Thomas Spragens, that Libertarians, classical liberals, and free market advocates are all linked intimately to atomistic individualism, which communitarians consider a false doctrine.

Interestingly, some in the classical liberal, Libertarian, and even the Objectivist movement, tend to make their own mistakes when they talk about "the market" as if were some entity that did some thinking of its own. Often some of these people say — maybe just as a short cut, but with some dire consequences — that the market did this and the market does that, as if there is some transcendent being with a mind, "the market". If you listen to financial analysts, for example, whenever there is a shift in the stock market, they talk as if the market is going about doing things on its own.

Let's go back a little bit and remember that one of the most important turns of events in the history of human thought occurred in England in the 17th century when Thomas Hobbes wrote his famous book, the *Leviathan*, in which he laid out a certain philosophical system in support of a conception of society that wasn't at that time yet a free society, but served as the grandparent of what later became, at the hands of Adam Smith and a lot of classical economists, the model of a free-market society. Hobbes had the notion that there really aren't any natures in realty. For example, there is no such thing as the nature of an apple, there's no such thing as the nature of a human being, nature of government, nature of leaves, trees, elephants, or anything. What we take to be the nature of something was, for Hobbes and his followers, a mere construct of our minds.

This was an interesting turn of events and can be explained because during the Middle Ages, when Aristotle's impact on Western culture was rather minimal and Plato's was substantial — and when even what was present of Aristotle's thought was re-introduced by Aquinas into Western culture with certain elements of Platonism — the nature of a thing was deemed to be out of this world, in a spiritual realm, and timeless and perfect. In other words, the idea of the nature of something meant some final firm static perfect form in a realm outside of the actual world in which we live. It's a little bit like you think about some mathematicians think about a circle or a square or a triangle. No actual triangle is actually quite triangular because if you look at any triangular thing or circular thing you'll always see that there are flaws in it. So there must be some standard of circularity — there must be some realm where there is a perfect circle and what geometers talk about. When one studies geometry one never studies any particular circle, one studies the supposed perfect circle. In Plato's vision in the way in which we understand the world, everything has this perfect version — human beings, zebra, cup of coffee, justice, whatever — and the task of philosophy, the task of dialectical inquiry, is to ultimately become so familiar with this perfect version of these particular kinds of things that we would have true knowledge. Only, as Socrates teaches, such knowledge is unavailable to us.

A lot of thinkers realized eventually that this objective that Plato laid out for us to seek leads to skepticism, cynicism, and nihilism because given that we the knower are temporal beings, given that we have to know things *in time*, we could never get to know something that is a-temporal, timeless. Skeptics thus got the upper hand and pointed out that with this model for what the nature of something is — including the nature of a human being — we can't know the nature of anything, including the human being.

Eventually Hobbes and his followers constructed an alternative approach to what is the nature of something. Since the Platonized Aristotelian conception of the nature of something was untenable, we had to have a substitute account of how we manage to say something about "appleness" as distinct from what we may say about any particular apple. Hobbes actually contended that the nature of something is conventional — it's invented by us. It's not real the way in which Plato seems to have thought — not even in the way that Aristotle thought, namely a good rational classification of something in a particular distinctive group like human beings in the human group, apples in the apple group, justice in the group of just things. No, these are all inventions; these are conventional in the sense in which for example it is conventional when I started writing this paper. It could have been some other time but I decided that it would be at, say, 3:30 PM. Along such lines, according to Hobbes we simply agreed to lump human beings together and call them human and their human nature namely the short cut to what it is to be human, is simply something we make up for our convenience, Not because it's so in reality, so in reality there is no nature of anything, in reality then what is left? Here is where the individualism emerged — this is where it took a very big hold on western civilization.

The reality that is left is what is called "bare particulars" — absolutely unique unclassifiable bit and pieces of reality. There are no glasses — there is just that glass that we happen to classify with other glasses, but as far as the reality is concerned, there's only that one thing and everything that really exists that has a true reality is of this kind — a pure individual. There are no natures — no rational classifiable things — there is only conventionally classified utterly idiosyncratic unique beings. This is what constituted a metaphysical foundation of individualism in the modern era. But that's not the only place this individualism made its appearance.

At the birth of Christianity, there was a sect of Christians, as discussed in Paul Zweig's *The Heresy of Self Love* (1958) who thought that God was the individual — in other words, that they were each gods. They didn't believe in any human nature — every god that they are individually is a wholly idiosyncratic, an utterly unique being.

The reason that this version of Christianity did not persist, is that eventually it led to complete chaos amongst the believers. Their view was like that of the 19th century radical individualist Max Sterner who believed that an individual is a totally idiosyncratic being and that it can do anything it wants, lacking any rules or principles pertaining to how it ought to conduct itself. There is no law; there is no rule, no guideline, and no ethics to guide the individual since the individual is wholly unique and conforms to nothing, not even its nature as a certain kind of being. Therefore, these Christians became extreme hedonists.

Now this is exactly what classical liberals are charged with by the communitarians — that by embracing the sort of individualism that we inherited through several generations and some alterations from Thomas Hobbes, we actually foster a kind of reckless hedonistic anarchic craziness. When Karl Max criticized the market place, he said he it was anarchic — meaning that in the market place of free competition and free enterprise, anybody was free to do whatever came to his mind. And accordingly there can be no justification for any criticism of anyone's conduct because the legacy of the individualism in modern economics leaves us without any objective values. All values are mere preferences.

It's interesting to note that Milton Friedman, who is one the heroes and probably one of the most respectable members of the classical liberal community in the 20th/21st century actually considers the free society simply his preference. He can't support it ethically because as he sees it there can be no objective "ethics" only subjective preferences. In this essentially Hobbesian tradition of individualism all judgments of what is good a bad or right and wrong are simply testimonials to what you like. As Hobbes himself put the point,

> But whatsoever is the object of any man's appetite or desire, that is it which he for his part calleth good: and the object of his hate and aversion, evil ... For these words of good and evil ... are ever used with relation to the person that useth them: there being nothing simply and absolutely so; nor any common rule of good and evil ... (Leviathan, Chapter 6, "Good"; Collier, p. 48.)

This is because without a nature, what would provide you with a standard for saying what is good for you or something is bad for you? Nothing. Anything goes. This is indeed the gist of the sort of individualism that a great deal of classical liberals have inherited and critics target with the hope that by discrediting individualism the entire idea of a free society in the classical liberal tradition will have been discredited. This version of individualism does have serious liabilities. Here are a few of them. First is the idea that human self is totally indeterminate — it's just some happenstance — your self is not a human self, not a dog self, not a Libertarian self, but any self you happen to want. You can classify yourself anyway in which you want and it will all be quite correct simply because that is what you choose it to be. You may not be in accord with others, but since their classification is purely conventional, arbitrary, why shouldn't yours be? It has just as much standing as anybody else. They only have larger numbers behind them. It's kind of a — this sort of individualism also encourages sort of a reckless wild self indulgence where you go to somebody and say that's not the right way to act — who's to say? You've heard this one many times and it's kind of an adolescence that speaks through classical liberalism Hobbesian tradition of individualism. There is no one to say — it's as if it's a matter of just saying, not knowing, not discovering, not objectively identifying what is right and wrong. Even more devastating is that our — I've already mentioned this with respect to the lat Milton Friedman — that our preference for a free society can be dismissed as merely our preference. Without any better standing than the preference of others for an unfree society. So we have no argument by which to defend our choice of liberty as opposed to our choice of slavery. A contemporary philosopher, Richard Rorty, made this very clear in an essay that he wrote for *The New Republic*. This was back in the time when there was a Soviet Union and he made the point that the standing that they have against democracy and the standing that we have for it, are just two different standings. As he put it, "Non-metaphysicians [of whom Rorty and, by his account, all other wise men are members] cannot say that democratic institutions reflect a moral reality and that tyrannical regimes do not reflect one, that tyrannies get something wrong that democratic societies get right." (Rorty, 1991)

There's nothing better or worse about either. It is a position that has been part of modern thinking as well as throughout human history. In our time it appears in deconstructionism and post modernism wherein not even words have any standards for meaning. If you use a word, you can mean anything you wish with it. When you are listening to me, my words just happen to be something that we have agreed to use to mean the things that I'm saying, but that's purely arbitrary, too.

So there's a great deal of liability with this radical subjectivist individualism — it leads to a reckless anarchy about everything. Yet the critics of this form of individualism don't actually have a lot to complain about because its liabilities are not all that bad — it is at most a misstep, like a glove that's a bit too large yet still does better than no glover or one too small. So assume that it is true and implies that people may be hedonistic, do what they want to do, and liberty is just a preference — all of this has its downsides but it is far less bad than what collectivism gives us. But it scares people. So from a point of view of the dialectics of argumentation, of trying to defend individualism in newspapers, magazines, books, and so on, the liability of this problematic form of individualism is serious for classical liberals — for people who want to live in a free society. Because it ultimately makes that choice arbitrary, groundless. If that's all there is, then we're just shouting at the other side in this debate. We have nothing really to offer to defend our position as "right" — it is simply a position we happen to like.

The question that arises then is, does this spell the death of individualism — given it's liabilities, its questionable pedigree, of how many people find it very awkward — maybe even impossible — to defend it philosophically, and how in some ways it is really counter intuitive — that is, by common sense assessment it is clear that nobody is an atom, a purely independent self (we are all born into families, we are all quite dependent until late in our lives on these families, we all tie ourselves to others even after we have grown legally mature, we indeed survive and flourish largely in communities — is that perhaps not a decisive reason to say that individualism is not only flawed but should be discarded as pointless?

Let me tell you the answer that both the left and the right give is exactly that. The left wants to dismiss it in favor of a coming worldwide cabal in which we hold hands together and sing hosannas in unison. The right thinks that this individualism is arrogant, that it is defiance of God, that it's in defiance of authority, excellence, and nobility and we should give it up for that reason. The Left construes individualism an enemy of community and solidarity, of human bonding, or belonging and a promoter of alienation, dehumanization. In short, both the right and the left are equally opposed to the classical liberal tradition — they are anti-individualist in a big and very confident way.

Part of the problem is that the most respected voices defending individualism in almost all cultures — and I'm sure it's so in New Zealand as well as in the US and in Canada, Europe — are the economists. Philosophical defenders of the free society have been marginalized and now that Nozick is dead, we'll experience another era of marginalization unless we are very lucky and work very, very hard.

So given that this is the case, there is very little in the way of respect for, concern about, even speculation about a possible successful form of individualism, maybe the damn thing ought to be discarded and we ought to go back to defending freedom on utilitarian grounds that it's "if people are free—even though they don't deserve to be—even there's no particular reason why they should be, nevertheless their freedom tends to produce the greatest happiness for the greatest number"—and that should be our only reason for favoring freedom. Then when we find that perhaps that doesn't quite bring home the bacon for everybody, then we should start tinkering with it—which was basically John Maynard Keynes' answer to individualism—it's basically a utilitarian system, but if it doesn't always do the right thing we can introduce government and meddle with the society and thus sacrifice liberty for the greater good.

Individualism, however, is actually sound. Now "sound"—or "true"—does not mean timelessly, unalterably true but reflective of how we ought to live so far as we know now. It means true beyond a reasonable doubt. That's a distinction that perhaps many are not familiar with—as in the law someone can be convicted if found guilty beyond the reasonable doubt. It isn't necessary to find someone guilty beyond a shadow of a doubt—in other words in such a way that it couldn't be conceived that he is innocent. Beyond a reasonable doubt means that if there are grounds for doubt, grounds that are understandable by human beings who populate the world today, then the conclusion may not be reached with confidence but if no such doubts exist, the conclusion reached amounts to knowledge.

The conclusion about individualism is as firm as the conclusion we reach without a reasonable doubt. One could imagine, fantasize that individualism has faults—science fiction writers do this all the time. But there isn't any good reason for it. Here is why: It is arguable without reasonable doubt that human nature that Hobbes dismissed as untenable, because of the impossible requirement that Plato placed on our identifying it is as Aristotle suggested, the fact of our being rational animals. This is no invention, no mere convention, not just an agreement, but grounded in our observations and rational organization of nature—observations supervised by reasoning.

So, we begin the defense of individualism—one I call classical individualism—with a rehabilitation of the idea of the nature of something. Once the Platonic demands of what it has to be for something to have a nature are cast aside as they ought to be, then the concept of the nature of something stands secure, without liability. Having reintroduced that, we come to the particular nature that is of concern to us, human nature. What does human nature look like if we study human beings? At very quick hint to be somewhat empirical about it, take a look around you—look at all these human beings who are (I have sort of hinted, I haven't clearly established, but I've hinted) are classifiable as humans and yet look at them—they are all so different. They have different hair cuts, different attire, different ideas, different habits, different nationalities, different sexes, different ages—they have all these differences. Moreover, some of them are lazy and some of them are diligent, some of them are verbal, some of them are quiet—and on and on and on. So you now begin to appreciate that when it comes to human nature, one of the distinctive aspects of humanity is individuality. In sounds paradoxical; here is something that allows us to classify human beings under one umbrella—human nature—and yet when we study human nature, what we find is an interesting aspect of what we call human beings is that they have highly individualized existences. They do their own thing, for better and worse, but now their own thing can be evaluated by reference to this human nature, whereas in Hobbes, it couldn't be evaluated. A human being that has a nature of a human being can be judged to be better or worse in terms of that nature. How well does it realize that nature? How much does it fail to realize it? In many, many areas of life—which obviously we'll not chronicle here, we can tell that. We can do that in special areas, like being a speaker (you can sit there by the way, right now and judge me as a human being who has taken on the job of giving talks). Now you have a standard—if I drop my pen too much more, you can say he's a lousy speaker—he should pay more attention, right? This will not be arbitrary, this will not be just conventional, and this will be based on what it is to be a speaker who is a human being who has made a promise to do a particular job competently rather than sloppily. You go on with this sort of analysis and you will realize that there is individualism here, but not arbitrariness. There is another aspect of this individualism that comes through, not by observation so much as I did earlier suspect, but by a way of explaining our differences as enormous disagreements, not just right here in this room because maybe in this room, there's not that much disagreement, but if you look past this room, you immediately detect it.

That has to do with our free will. Now a lot of people dispute free will on grounds that they say modern science no longer admits of such a mythical concept — this is an inheritance of religion, that Kant, who is a religious person, tried to resurrect it but could never give it a natural footing so therefore the whole thing should be given up. But again it is a very difficult to make sense of what we do — of what you do right now — as for example you are listening to me and maybe trailing off into some vacation spot in Hawaii or whatnot, or thinking about how nice it would be having him off the podium and get someone more interesting here. You know all of these are all very creative things — and you can't explain these creative things without the concept of an agent — your agency. You are not just responding to me, I'm not just a stimulant, I'm actually someone being evaluated, assessed, judged by you and that can't make sense without the idea of free will. If you don't generate the thoughts in your mind, formulate the assessment that you give of whatever this is or the meal that you eat or the clothes that you have bought, and you now say, "what the hell did I do?" — what was I thinking? That very self-noticeable fact that you are constantly evaluating, reflecting, assessing, regretting — "Damn it, I didn't think", we say, suggests that we have a freedom that other parts of nature do not have.

The fact that we have it is not that strange. After all there are many other parts of nature that don't have things that other parts of nature have, so maybe we came into nature, through evolution or however, by having these distinctive features. We are individuals and we are also individuals who drive ourselves — who have, as I discuss in my book (which by the way the supervisor back there, has induced me to offer to sign in case you buy some, because we need more sales — so this is a sort of a pitch). Anyway this book lays out the notion that human beings have this unusual, but not unexplainable capacity for initiative — to take the initiative. Once that too is integrated with our understanding of individualism, you begin to see why it is not subjective to say that someone is failing to realize his or her full potential. It now signifies that that person has the capacity to either realize or fail to realize it. It is up to the person to do so and since it is up to the person to do so, blaming the person or praising the person now begins to make sense. On the other hand, if you are back to the Hobbes picture of individualism, then whatever individuals do, simply happens to them. There is no way to even criticize a tyrant, a Hitler, or a minor one like Ralph Nader, with doing anything wrong. Liberals, classical liberals, Libertarians would lose the ability to even be critical of those who deprive them of their freedom, their liberty — because all those people just have to do what they're doing. So we have now with the ingredient of free will, with the ingredient of individuality, a very good making of a morally significant human existence. Not just a human existence in which there are different preferences, different tastes, different ways in which people happen to move but a life in which human beings, unlike other beings, are responsible for what they do. This is a big element of individualism besides the fact that they are of course differently configured from birth on, but they are also differently able to — and willing to — operate in the world. There's another element of individuality — not only that you are, after all, an individual having different attributes from people next to you, or near you, or across the world, but also because you make different uses of those attributes — some wise, some unwise, some prudent, some reckless.

Here you introduce into an individualism that at first seems like recklessly anarchic — for more of a place for standards of evaluation, than collectivists could ever muster, because for the collectivists ultimately the standards are a matter of collective agreement. Individuals are always victims of this collective agreement. One of the reasons that you will find so many elements of our social life now dismissed as something beyond our control is that collectivists have not got a way to assign responsibility for conduct, but the individualist does.

It is interesting that Ayn Rand's *The Virtue of Selfishness* (1964) has a subtitle that is routinely overlooked when people give it a cursory glance. It's "A New Concept of Egoism" — a new concept. What is new about it?

It is precisely the classical element I've been calling attention to, the neo Aristotelian understanding of our nature, one that implies individuality. Any Rand was well aware that the old form of individualism — the one we associate with Hobbes and the 19th century with Max Sterner and in the 20th century with neoclassical and Austrian economists, is not quite a successful one — it doesn't truly identify what human nature is and what those individuals who have that nature are. She undertook to lay out what David Kelley calls an "unrugged" individualism that doesn't mean one has no moral restraints in one's life. No, an individual who does that is acting badly, engaging in misconduct, something that may be said truly by reference to our human nature.

At the end of the day we have here a humanized version of individualism rather than the dehumanized version that we have inherited in much of the classical liberal tradition and ultimately from Hobbes. In this connection I want to cite a passage by Tatiana Tolstoya. Tolstoya had this to say about collectivism, about what the collectivists claim and what the communitarians claim.

> Taken individually, in short, everyone is not good. Perhaps this is true, but then how did all these scoundrels manage to constitute a good people? The answer is that 'the people' is not 'constituted of.' According to [collectivists] 'the people' is a living organism, not a 'mere mechanical conglomeration of disparate individuals.' This, of course, is the old, inevitable trick of totalitarian thinking: 'the people' is posited as unified and whole in its multiplicity. It is a sphere, a swarm, an anthill, a beehive, a body. And a body should strive for perfection; everything in it should be smooth, sleek, and harmonious. Every organ should have its place and its function: the heart and brain are more important than the nails and the hair, and so on. If your eye tempts you, then tear it out and throw it away; cut off sickly members, curb those limbs that will not obey, and fortify your spirit with abstinence and prayer. (Tolstoya, 1992, p. 33.)

Now this is actually directly out of Marx; this is not a caricature of collectivism. She is not being unfair. In the *Grundrisse*, Marx's posthumously published book, it is clearly stated (on page 33) that humanity is an "organic body" (or "whole") that undergoes this dialectical development to reach its final realization in communism.

That view may not be fully embraced by communitarians or by welfare statists and so on, but it underlines their view — their general attitude is that we can sacrifice the business people for the artists or the scientists or the educators or those who are into drugs for the sake of the collective whole. That line of thinking can not be stopped if we stick to the old form of primitive individualism that we find in Thomas Hobbes. Unless we give a solid account of individualism — one that withstands criticism, one that can show itself to be true to what we mostly know about human beings, namely that — critics, such as the communitarians, will certainly be eager to throw out the baby with the bath-water.

Chapter IV

Liberty and Morality

[M]an acts from judgment, because by his apprehensive power
he judges that something should be avoided or sought. But
because this judgment, in the case of some particular act, is not
from a natural instinct, but from some act of comparison in the
reason, therefore he acts from free judgment and retains the
power of being inclined to various things. And forasmuch as
man is rational is it necessary that man have a free-will.

Thomas Aquinas, *Summa Theologica*, Q. 93

It is perhaps one of the most difficult aspects of a free society to
accept that others' immoral conduct may be interfered with by
peaceful means alone, namely, persuasion, propaganda, advocacy,
boycott or ostracism. This is a great strength as well as one of the
least popular aspects of the free society and of its political-philo-
sophical statement, libertarianism. It is therefore important to
address it — can champions of liberty rebut the charge that they are
promoting evil by making immoral conduct possible?

Let's consider the basic ingredient of the political theory of liberty,
what is now dubbed libertarianism. At its heart is the idea that in
human communities it is individuals who are sovereign — the people who rule ought to be the individuals who inhabit the community
and they are to rule only themselves unless they give permission to
someone else — as one might by letting a coach, body guard or trainer
order one about because one has authorized the person to do so.
That's one meaning of "the consent of the governed".

There is no class of rulers in a genuine free human community,
either designated by God or by history. Every human being has a
right to govern his or her own life. In fact, that's the best way to make
clear what this is about, is to remind ourselves of the crucial lines of
the United States Declaration of Independence: "We hold these
truths to be self evident, that all men are created equal and are
endowed by their creator with certain unalienable rights to life,

liberty, and the pursuit of happiness" and "that to secure these rights, governments are instituted."

Now, if one appreciates the full meaning of those lines, one will grasp quite clearly the crux of a free society. It is that the only job government can have in a just human community is to protect individual rights. That would involve having courts of law in which disputes about rights violations are adjudicated, via military that would defend the people from outside aggression, and there would be police that would defend people from criminal conduct. There would not be government sponsored radio or television stations, sports arenas and auditoriums, tennis courts and golf courses. All these would violate the strictures of a libertarian system of justice.

The reason for that is that all such projects, when carried out by governments, involve taking some peoples' property or labor and forcibly transferring their ownership or fruits to somebody else's. And that is not permitted in a free society to anyone, including even a democratically elected government, because a free society rests on the understanding that every individual has a right to his or her life, to his or her liberty, and to the pursuit of his or her happiness. Whatever goals one's life, actions or property are devoted to must be determined by one's own judgment and not by the judgments of some master, leading elite or group of politicians and bureaucrats — not even by "the majority".

It's amazing for some who have come to the United States from abroad — where these ideas were looked upon as dreams to be realized sometime in the future and only one country was seen to have come close to realizing them, named the United States — to discover what so many people who write about politics in the USA believe. Whether in academic journals, in books published by Harvard, Princeton and Stanford University Press, or on the editorial pages of newspapers, the original and quintessential American idea of individual rights to life, liberty and property is hardly respected, never mind embraced.

It is even embarrassing that today in the United States there are more prominent thinkers advocating collectivist alternatives like communitarianism, socialism, communism, even certain varieties of (democratic?) fascism, than there are almost anywhere else in the world. When people visit here from the former Soviet Union or Poland or Russia, they're often stunned how many of our professors in political philosophy and political science departments seem to favor a system that they have experienced and now generally find completely inadequate for the needs of a human communities.

Well, be that as it may, it should be made clear that the ideals that were sketched, and only sketched, in the Declaration of Independence are *radical*. That means these ideas go to the root of the basic issues of community life. That's why it's called the American *revolution*. It wasn't just that there was a lot of fighting going on at the country's beginning but that a certain idea of how governments ought to be understood had been fundamentally overturned via the official statement of the Founders of the republic.

The American founders rejected the top-down shape of society, one in which kings, monarchs, Caesar's, pharaoh's, czar's, would rule subjects. The founders have come upon the notion that there is something fundamentally amiss in a community in which certain people enjoy what is thought to be a naturally superior status to others and can use others as their resources for their various goals. What happened is that instead of seeing the king, the state or the government as the sovereign while the inhabitants of the community as *subjects* — as they're still called in Canada, Australia, New Zealand and England because they are subject to the will of the king (even if it's mostly ceremonial now) — the official political philosophy of the country was to be that individuals are sovereign (independent and self-ruling). In the United States of America what had been substituted for the top down idea of government is the recognition that all of us individually have dominion over ourselves: Our lives are for us to direct, for better and for worse. This is individualism and it meant to unseat feudalism, one variety of collectivism.[1]

Now this is very difficult for many people to accept, namely, that a person's life is his or her own, for better or for worse. That is because throughout recorded history most official political outlooks taught something very different. Human beings were supposed to belong to the clan, tribe, country, family, ethnic group, racial or social class, or the nation. Even in our day the idea that the community owns the individual — that it is to the community that one *belongs* — is widely promulgated (Taylor, 1989).

In a bona fide free society individuals have the right to their own lives, their own liberty, and their own pursuit of happiness, which

---

[1]   It isn't being claimed here that all of the Founders were libertarians. What is true, however, is that they put their political ideas in terms that eventually gave rise to a fully developed libertarian political philosophy. This is because they had been influenced by classical liberals such as John Locke. For more on this see Machan (2001).

means that you have to accept that your next door neighbor, in fact all the people in your community, have the right to act in ways that may even be quite improper. If they choose to ruin themselves with drug or alcohol abuse, or if they work for causes that are trivial and meaningless, there is nothing anyone is authorized to do to them apart from imploring them to change their ways. They may be spending their lives and resources on goals that are morally abhorrent or silly, yet this is their right to do and no one may prevent it from happening by means other than persuasion.[2]

The point needs to be stressed: It isn't just that if we do not like or prefer or approve of how they act, they may not be intruded upon but that *they have a right to do what is, in fact, morally wrong*. There may well be people who are racists, bigots, lazy, or wrong in many others ways in how they guide their own lives and one isn't able to reach them by way of argument—influence them with books about their errors and vices, successfully editorialize against them, or boycott them—yet they may not be forced to change. There is no justification for one to go treat them as if they were one's children and make them act as one judges, possibly quite correctly, to be correct. As Abraham Lincoln put the point, "No man is good enough to govern another man, without that other's consent."[3]

This is the crucial aspect of a free society. Of course, many of us, quite rightly, become very exercised about the misbehavior of our fellow human beings, often to the point where we urge vice-squad action against them by government. Such misbehavior tends to have an adverse impact—albeit not via force but osmosis—on the lives of those near the perpetrators. So many would naturally like to prevent this.[4]

---

[2]   Immoral conduct that infringes on or violates others' rights may, of course, be rebuffed but not because it is immoral but because it invades the moral sphere of another.

[3]   The full quote goes as follows: "No man is good enough to govern another man without that other's consent. When a man governs himself, that is self-government; but when he governs himself and also governs another man, then that is more than self- government—that is despotism. Our reliance is in the love of liberty, which God has planted in us; our defense is in the spirit which prizes liberty as the heritage of all men in all lands, everywhere. Those who deny freedom to others deserve it not for themselves, and under a just God cannot long retain it."
      http://www.carpenters.org/history/century_0798.html

[4]   Those who champion the polity of individual liberty do not deny such influences but note that they are not independent of the choices of those

If a racist refuses to deal with people of a different race, some of what the racist has to offer to people, from which they could benefit, is not going to be forthcoming to those people. That is lamentable, upsetting, and some people find this intolerable and want to use the government to remedy it. Drug abuse, lack of ambition and prudence, failure to act generously and the like are all targeted for remedy this way by those who find it a serious problem that people aren't always doing the right thing for themselves and for others. The result of this is often the enactment of laws and public policies that promise to correct the situation, direct those concerned to behave better, do the right thing.

When government responds to the urgings of vocal constituents to make people behave, it is difficult to raise the issue that this isn't what government is supposed to do. It is easier to see how wrong this is when the behavior being imposed is not decent, not commendable, as when government kept slavery and segregation in force. And when it was finally widely recognized that these institutions are wrong and should be illegal, government was in part instrumental in ending them. The only notable example of halting government from trying to make people behave well is prohibition. So this makes it appear that government is the proper instrument for undoing all bad things — or promoting all good things — in a human communities. A lot of people see that gambling is bad for many who engage in it, or prostitution and the reading of Hustler Magazine. If they had their way they would have the government intrude and make all this better.

But, and here is the crux of the issue, that would itself be morally wrong and more — it would also be invasive and thus may be resisted.[5] Human adults are not to be treated in such a manner by their government, an agency that ought not to conduct itself in ways it had been thought proper once (and is still thought proper in many regions of the globe), namely, paternalistically.

It is wrong to empower some people to try to make other people good. Coercion is not how adults ought to deal with one another. It is precisely the hallmark of civilization that one must convince people to change their ways. One of the clearest signs of a free society is that it adheres to an ideal of civilized intercourse. This means that the

who are being influenced, thus they may not be forcibly warded off, only via education, persuasion, and other peaceful means.

[5] This point, stressed about governments that are tyrannical, is made clear in the Declaration of Independence and powerfully lends that document its libertarian flavor.

methods appropriate to human beings rather than to beasts rule community life. One does not remedy others' conduct with violence and force. One has to approach them by reasoning, arguing with them and by trying to persuade them. And if that doesn't work, one has to live with it. The most one can do is ostracize such people, leave them be on their own and suffer the consequences of their ways. And only if their misconduct is intrusive, in violation of one's rights, may one use defensive force to fend them off.[6]

Trying to *make* others good by means of prohibiting their choices from taking effect, that is, via prohibition, or by forcing them to do the right thing — that is regimentation — is also a futile effort. That's because ethical, morally good, human conduct has to be the outcome of the choice or initiative of the agent who is to perform it.[7] If I don't choose to be decent but am made to behave that way by others, this will not make me decent. Morally upright conduct has to be voluntary. No amount of coercion will achieve my generosity, compassion, charity, honesty, prudence or temperance. Force, indeed, may only be used defensively — and most of us realize this when we consider that self-defense justifies its use even while nothing else does.

There is some evidence of the recognition of this libertarian approach to community life present in the American legal system. For example, the Federal Constitution — in what turns out to be unjustly discriminatory fashion — largely protects the individual liberty of journalists, book publishers, writers, ministers of churches and the like.[8] They do not in most cases have to conform to standards of right conduct or even the majority's will. They are most often legally protected from government making any decision as to how they should behave. There is no Department of Journalism at the Federal, State, County, or Municipal level. Journalists don't have to go through licensing or board certification with any branch of level of government in order to be eligible for work in their profession.

That is because it was understood by the founders very clearly — so clearly that they wanted to write it down and enact it into major

---

[6]   This, incidentally, is one crucial reason so many among the political leaders of many authoritarian, including theocratic foreign countries (and the supporters among the clergy and intellectuals) find America detestable. Its system refuses to take over the management of citizens who mismanage their own lives.

[7]   For a fuller story on this point, see Machan (2000).

[8]   Unjustly discriminatory because members of other professions are coerced for various precautionary, preventive purposes, while journalists and ministers are exempt from this treatment. This certainly violates the spirit if not the letter of the 14th Amendment to the US Constitution.

law — that human beings may not be made to think differently from the way they *choose* to think. As much as their thinking may well be wrong — as much the fact that some people decide to join the Communists Party, the Aryan Nation or some satanic cult — their actions are not properly subject to being commandeered. Neither their thinking, nor their actions — for example their devotion of all of their resources to such organizations and their objectives — may be subject to regimentation. Baptists might be upset that some people worship god differently from how they worship and that they devote their resources and time to this kind of worship. Yet, in a free society no one gets to commandeer their thinking and their behavior, at least not with respect to how they should worship or what sort of ideas they should propagate in their newspapers and their books.

Now, this is strange. Is it not important for journalists and authors and ministers of churches to be free, including to be free to write and preach bad ideas? It surely looks like it, considering that yellow journalism, for examples, is not banned in this country. It exists all around.

But if it is OK for journalists and ministers and the faithful to be free to think and act as they see fit, it is curious that it's not OK for some people to do what they want to do — for example, to gamble, get involved in prostitution or bad advertising. Why are those people, the professionals in journalism and in religion, protected from other people's commandeering their behavior, while others are not protected? That is wrong.

The libertarian sees it differently. Basically, let us generalize the principles that are embedded in the First Amendment to the Constitution to everything — for example, education, medicine, automobile works and the rest. There should be a complete separation of state and all the professions. Government ought not to be permitted to regiment any of them.

Take the hard case of education, hard because so many people are used to sending their kids to publicly funded, compulsory schools and have gotten comfortable about it all. First, it is wrong to confiscate funds from some people in order to educate the children of other people. Second, it is wrong to commandeer young people to accept one particular type of education that is handed down by a particular government bureaucracy. There should be as much variety in education as there is in magazines or newspapers. There should be as much diversity there. Children are individuals, too. They should not be herded into classrooms and treated as if they all had the very same needs, the same aptitudes, the same talent. There should be attention to the diversity of children just as there is attention to the diversity of our nutritional needs. There are many, many different types of restaurants, the government is not in a restaurants business. There are many, many different types of department stores, the government is not in a department store business and for good reason, because there are very, very different needs.

Human beings share a few things amongst each other; they are all rational animals. They have certain biological similarities and they are all capable of thinking. But, how they will put this thinking to use in their lives, that will differ a great deal. That depends upon their circumstances, their background, their talent, their physique, all kinds of things. Just look around. All your neighbors are human beings and yet every one is different from the other. They all have certain idiosyncratic ways of being. And these are what a free society respects.

Not that there is no bad behavior that needs to be remedied, corrected, improved, of course there is. There is not only innocently different behavior but also outright bad behavior, even apart from the behavior that should be illegal, namely, when some invade the lives of others. That is the only bad behavior that should be prohibited by government, punished if it occurs, the sort that forcibly intrudes on the lives of others. If you write an editorial criticizing another person, that other person can ignore that editorial and walk away. So can one ignore another's gambling, drug abuse and prostitution. But, if one intrudes on another's home, breaks in, burglarizes it, or perpetrates an assault, kidnapping, rape or murder, that's something that should be resisted. The reason that governments are instituted amongst human beings, clearly understood by the American founders—something that libertarians extend into many other areas of human life—is that we need a specialized agency, trained to deploy due process, so as to deal with violent intruders into our lives.

The reason that we need a specialized agency—that even in the process of dealing with violent intruders (that is, with a criminal suspect)—is that those suspects are human beings and interacting with them requires certain rules that respect their humanity. That's the point of due process in the criminal law. You can't simply just shoot someone's head off because he steals a couple of pennies from you. You cannot intrude on a person in response to his intrusion without observing the fact that this is a human being and this human being has rights. Just as this is a model in the criminal law, so it should be in all human interaction. You cannot deal with people violently even if you thoroughly disagree with their way of life. Even if you consider their way of life abhorrent.

Oddly, what is generally understood to apply to criminal suspects is not applied to members of professions outside those covered by the First Amendment. Other professionals may be burdened with all kinds of regulations, fees and the like even though no proof exists that they have done anything wrong to anyone. The mere possibility of their doing something wrong suffices to impose upon them such undeserved burdens.

The United States may loosely be called a democracy, but in fact it was meant to be a constitutional democracy. A constitutional democracy basically means something very similar to a constitutional monarchy. Both restrict the powers of government. According to the Declaration of Independence's principles, democracy may not be used to transfer wealth from one party to another party. It may not be used to decide for all of us what kind of life we are supposed to lead. Some of this is also captured in the US Constitution, as well as many state constitutions.

And why is this so? Why is that of some significance? Why is this supposed to be right rather than simply a tradition that happened to grow up in America?

Well, that's a serious and complex philosophical issue. Certainly, there is an assumption underlying this kind of government pertaining to human nature. It is the view that one owns one's life and that another may not rule this life. It assumes that everyone has his or her own task in guiding one's life and that we are all free agents and how we perform that task is going to be what determines our fundamental moral character, the quality of our lives, something that we ought to determine and where intrusion is impermissible unless we say otherwise. The individual person is supposed to be the one who determines whether he or she lives a good or bad life, whether one is rewarded for this in this world or in another. This is not something others may take over, as if we were children whose parents may treat us as dependents and minors.

It is this idea of us being fundamentally free agents, choosing beings, that necessitates these principles of individualism. Individual rights make sense because we need a sphere of jurisdiction, of personal authority, where our decisions count and significantly influence outcomes. So that when we are judged — either by ourselves, by our friends, or by history — we can be judged accurately.

If, however, we are all herded together like conscripts, then what we do is really not our doing. It is the doing of the masters above us, or of the government or of the majority. If you are made to pay for some policy the government has, either democratically or quasi-democratically — which is more likely the case — decided it should be carried out and you are made to fund it, when foreigners say, "Look what your country is doing. It is supporting this particular regime with foreign aid, with military aid, with all sorts of stuff but depriving others of the same and is thus making very controversial, often wrong, decisions", can you really accept responsibility for that? If the resources have been coercively taken from citizens, this cannot be their doing. Citizens are all then just members of a conscripted crowd.

There was a time when even some prominent Americans realized all of this. One day many moons ago, in the US House of Representatives, a bill was taken up appropriating money for the benefit of a widow of a distinguished naval officer. Several beautiful speeches had been made in its support. The Speaker was just about to put the question when Crockett arose:

> Mr. Speaker — I have as much respect for the memory of the deceased, and as much sympathy for the sufferings of the living, if suffering there be, as any man in this House, but we must not permit our respect for the dead or our sympathy for a part of the living to lead us into an act of injustice to the balance of the living. I will not go into an argument to prove that Congress has no power to appropriate this money as an act of charity. Every member upon this floor knows it. We have the right, as individuals, to give away as much of our own money as we please in charity; but as members of Congress we have no right so to appropriate a dollar of the public money. Some eloquent appeals have been made to us upon the ground that it is a debt due the deceased. Mr. Speaker, the deceased lived long after the close of the war; he was in office to the day of his death, and I have never heard that the government was in arrears to him.
>
> Every man in this House knows it is not a debt. We cannot, without the grossest corruption, appropriate this money as the payment of a debt. We have not the semblance of authority to appropriate it as a charity. Mr. Speaker, I have said we have the right to give as much money of our own as we please. I am the poorest man on this floor. I cannot vote for this bill, but I will give one week's pay to the object, and if every member of Congress will do the same, it will amount to more than the bill asks.

Some would argue that such charitable deeds can be performed democratically, but that is a mistake. To start with, there's always the problem that in regimented committees and large groups—unless you join these groups freely and you have what economists refer to as the exit option, that is the option to leave the group and not be part of it—you cannot be held responsible for what the group does unless you have freely consented to the method by which decisions are reached. Otherwise you're just a conscript in this group. That's one of the central dangers of extending democracy too far in community affairs.

When democracy works, for example in the Kwanias Club or in a Rotary Club and so on, that's because people sign up for the democratic process as they join or enter the door. They know this is the case, so when democracy is practiced, there can be no basic complaint.. But when one is born into a community, it is not the case that one may be forced to submit to the democratic process. It is no excuse saying, "Well, you were born here, so you have to adhere to the democratic process." What if the person wouldn't choose to do that? What if his or her judgement precluded submitting all the issues to a democratic method? They ought to be free to make that choice. And if we respected their fundamental humanity as free agents, who have responsibilities to carry out in their lives, then we would recognize this right to freedom and we would enshrine it into law and protect it just as the Declaration declared that it should be protected.

There is one principle that libertarians take very seriously, indeed. It is not uncontroversial but they have reached a state of mind in line with which this is a principles that is certain beyond any reasonable doubt.

The libertarian maintains that individual human beings are sovereign. They are not subject, by any justification, to the rule of other individuals unless they have given their consent. This is the meaning of the concept of the consent of the governed.

Human beings are free-judging agents. They need to have this recognized in law and the libertarian basically advocates a political society in which this is done through and through.

Now, let me say something about the future of this libertarian outlook. Nobody pretends that overnight there will come into being a libertarian society. No champion of individual rights can be that hopeful. Most of us realize that a great many people are so wedded to government hand outs and powers promising to solve problems they think need urgent solutions and they're so well accustomed to governments making such promises to them, that they are almost unable to see any other alternative. When it comes to the environment, well it has to be the government that does it. When it comes to AIDS research, it has to be the government. They don't even imagine any longer, even for the sake of argument, just as an exploration, what it would be like to leave matters like that to the voluntary choices of members of the society rather than to the forceful imposition of governments.

Most of us who champion liberty recognize all this. However, we are also aware that if we do not continue with our efforts — if we do not make our voices heard in the community, if we do not capitalize on the few people who are willing to entertain the possibility and maybe even the likelihood of the emergence of a genuine free society — then this beacon of liberty in human history called the United States of America is going to degenerate into a demagogic, despotic, society. So, at least, we may be holding back something that would bring back the ways of Caesar, of the czars, or of George III. That alone is with the effort, as far as I can grasp these matters.

Chapter V*

What's Worst About Taxation

And What can Take its Place?

To begin with, a sketch of the history of taxation. If you reflect upon it, you probably know from your own study of American as well as world history that up until about 200 years ago most states, nations, governments, countries and other organized communities were more or less absolute monarchies. In other words, they were owned by a king or queen and his or her entourage. There's a lot of this still left, mostly at the ceremonial level but often for quite real. For example, there is a monarchy in Great Britain, Norway, Denmark or Sweden. The monarchs live very well, but they don't have too much political power any longer. Elsewhere, however, such as Syria or Saudi Arabia the monarchical system is in full and serious force.

One of the ways in which one can measure the progress of civilization is by the erosion of the absolute power of monarchies; czars, pharos, caesars, kings and such. The distinctive element of the American Revolution, the Declaration of Independence, was to overthrow, effectively, the operations of a monarchy on this continent. In other words, what did the Declaration do? It identified the individual citizen, as opposed to the king, as the sovereign in a country. Sovereign means self-rule. Sovereignty is self-rule.

What is distinctive about the American political tradition — actually established in England and France but declared as official public philosophy in the USA — is that instead of treating the inhabitants of a society as subjects — that is, subject to the rule of the king — they were henceforth to be treated as sovereign, self-rulers, whose

---

* Some portions of this chapter are based on Machan (1982).

consent to be governed was required for the government to be legitimate.

Previous to this declaration, although the idea surfaced here and there in the minds of political thinkers, this idea had never risen to official public policy. It was never implemented as the rule of law. The Americans, however, went on record attempting to implement it as the rule of law. They didn't do it consistently. They tolerated slavery in their Constitution, for example, and they continued a number of other policies from the old era, among them the institution of taxation.

Now, with the rule of the monarch the idea was that anyone who worked in the country — on the land or anywhere else — enjoyed a privilege and would have to pay for that. No one was understood to have a right to work. Instead, they got permission to work and for that permission they had to pay a price which was taxation. It was a kind of rent one had to pay and a lot of economists still refer to some of these things as rent. In fact, however, "rent" is a misnomer here, since what is meant by it is "freely negotiated payment for use." Instead, taxation is akin to extortion: You must pay if you want to do what you have a right to do, what no one may stop you from doing, namely, engage in productive activities.

If you may hire out your skills and time only provided you pay me, a party not involved in the employment relationship, 5 cents for each hour you work, and if I have the power to enforce this, what am I doing? I'm engaging in extortion. When we identify the conduct of criminals, as they confiscated payments from people who do not owe anything to them, as extortion, we do this because the criminals are taking payments for something they were not contracted to do for anyone. To then penalize the victim is extortion, not rent.

Presumably, however, in a society in which the individual inhabitants are sovereign, you don't have to pay me for the privilege of working at whatever you can be voluntarily employed to do. But, if I own you — or own the land off which you live — then I can confiscate such payment from you. Taxation was the confiscation of such payment.

Farmers had to pay their lords — their court appointed masters — this fee in order to be able to live and work there. They did not have the right of private property, for example. They could not acquire land for themselves because the land belonged to the king and his nobles. The only thing they could do is to obtain the king's permission to live and work on the land. And once they sold the harvest, part of their take was taken to belong to the king.

Indeed, whatever the king said, they had to pay him. That is what in the modern sense amounts to extortion. In the older sense it was called rent because the king was assumed to be the genuine, legitimate owner of the country. All the people whom he or she empowered to manage various parcels of the country — mainly members of the nobility — then lived off this rent.

You can understand this if you understand anything about private property rights, if you have something that is your private property and someone else wants to make use of it, you can set the terms of the use. You can say, you may use the property provided you pay me something or provided you whistle a song for me or provided you give me your children or something like that, you know? Then the people either get away from there, move someplace else if they can afford to, or they have to come up with this payment.

On the other hand, if you accept the legitimacy of the Revolution that was accomplished in the Declaration of Independence at the federal level and at the various state levels and various constitutions and Bill of Rights, then you can understand that maybe the institution of taxation is itself suspect. Morally and politically suspect. And ought, perhaps, to be legally reformed. I mean, seriously reformed. None of this band-aid reform that every year occurs with the politicians saying, well we'll take out this passage and substitute another passage and put in this loop-hole then take out that loop-hole which is the current tax reform. Every time you see tax reform it's just basically a revamping of the redistributionist nature of taxation. Some people get more taxes, some people get less taxes and this changes, but the fundamental question of whether taxation is itself consistent with the American revolutionary political outlook, indeed, whether it is just at all, doesn't get raised except by a few people who tend to be marginalized. It doesn't get raised in public finance circles or the forums, such as scholarly journals, textbooks, and so on, where the topic of public finance is studied.

Some of this is understandable if not excusable. There is a lethargy about extending the revolutionary ideas that far because most people don't comprehend how the functions that a government of a free society is recognized to have to perform could be funded without taxation. (In fact, some who defend the free society have elected to call themselves anarchists in part because they, too, do not fathom how government could be voluntarily funded.)

Most people, then, take taxation to be a necessary, if not consistent, component of a society, even one with a free legal system. Judges have to be paid, as do the police, military and so forth. Even the most minimal form of government, the type, for example, that a libertarian endorses, has to be financed. There is no way to just get money from heaven for the government to be able to feed itself and to function.

Since, however, there is no extension of the notion of self-rule into the area of public funding, most people are just silent about the subject of taxation's inconsistency with freedom.

It is a difficult issue. Most people take it that a government or legal authority is such a vital part of a community that funding it must be guaranteed. Perhaps nourishment doesn't need to be financed, maybe you don't need to fund clothing, maybe medical services will just be delivered free of charge but governments must be funded, no matter what. Of course, once government gets involved in procuring these other provisions, they too seem to require a guarantee.

As a fact of the history of ideas, there has been a good deal of dispute about whether governments are really absolutely necessary for society. Some people have argued, for example, that if you tally up the crimes that have been committed in the history of humanity, the most ferocious criminals have been governments. They have carried out most of the wars, built the concentration camps, established the gulags, carried out the purges and the rest. None of this could have occurred without the massive concentrated force that is part and parcel of government.

In democratic or, more or less individualist systems of politics, governments tend to be justified on the basis that they are needed for the defense of human rights threatened by domestic criminals and foreign aggression. That's the justification of government. If you look at the US Declaration of Independence, which is rather skeptical about governments in their traditional form, it says — just after it says that we hold these truths to be self-evident, that all men are created equal and are endowed by their creator with certain unalienable rights, amongst them life, liberty and the pursuit of happiness — that governments are instituted to secure these rights. Governments are not instituted to provide AIDS research or to build monuments to dead politicians or to preserve historical buildings. Going to hairdressers is important to many people but to argue that it should be subsidized by taxpayers would be absurd, even today.

But there are a lot of things that are comparable to getting a hairdo that are being subsidized by government.

For example, American firms that advertise abroad have half of their advertising paid for by American taxpayers. Why? They have simply managed to lobby that into law. They have the capacity to lobby politicians who have the willingness to sell their services to special interest groups. Some of these may be very worthy projects but that's not what governments are instituted for. Human beings ought to be free to live their lives on terms they choose, which includes spending their wealth as they see fit, not as the employees of the government order them to. The proper function of the government is to do work when other people (are about to) attack citizens, not when nature or one's own errors deliver upon one untoward conditions. Nature does harm us frequently—we are attacked by viruses, we get colds, minor and major diseases, floods, hurricanes, tornadoes and earthquakes wreak havoc on our lives but these aren't political matters at all. We have all sorts of problems not perpetrated by other people against whom government is supposed to provide us with protection.

At one time all these matters had been the province of politics—it was the role of the king and its court to guard all aspects of the realm over which he or she ruled. That's because it was understood that the king owns the realm with the rest being his or her subjects, not sovereign citizens.

Unfortunately, that relationship between citizens and government is being resurrected and now many people look to government to solve all their problems. Thus, all of our problems have become political. Their solution then must be funded and so as to finance this it is absolutely necessary that the government reclaim its earlier power of expropriation, that is, the authority to conscript labor and property so it'd be available to use by the government for all the problem solving tasks it now has.

If the government followed its job description, in line with the individualist political tradition that emerges from the America Revolution—whereby individuals have to give their consent if they are to be governed—then we'd find that the notion of funding the government apart from taxation no longer becomes so alien. Then we could open the questions as to whether there are some ways of doing it.

But before this happens it is necessary that it be understood that the criticism of taxation is that it is taking what belongs to people without their consent. It's taking without permission.

Notice the founders kind of thought of this because in the 5th Amendment to the US Constitution and the Bill of Rights, they make reference to under what circumstances the government may take your property. It is only for public use and even then with full compensation.

The concept of "public use" in a properly limited, individualist political order includes only the spheres required to administer the law, which involves securing our rights to life, liberty and the pursuit of happiness. It isn't just anything about which some loud enough portion of the public is upset. Within the framework of a polity that is governed according to the principles of individual rights, "public use" means matters such as administering courts, the military and the police. Perhaps roads and the Post Office were thought of explicitly, too, but that's about it. It certainly does not include everything that some segment of the population doesn't like solving on its own but wants the government to solve for it.

So, if you restrict this notion of public use, even to what the founders meant by it, you would have definitive objection against nearly all of government taxation, not to mention eminent domain and others types of unjust takings perpetrated by politicians these days. (Just consider the millions of acres of land presidents simply declare to be "public", with no justification at all in terms recognizable in the US Constitution.)

Under the bloated definition of public use, where it means anything some portion of the public gets away with getting the government to do for them, there is an enormous public sphere. It is one of the sources of the problems courts have with applying the Bill of Rights today — for example, public schools run up against the First Amendment if they allow prayer or exercise editorial control over students newspapers. This would not happen if school were private.

Nearly everything now is public. One reason, for example, that the government in California could prohibit private restaurants and bars from having smoking sections is that legally they claim that these private restaurants and bars were tied in with the public interest. How? Because they open on to the public roads.

In fact if this line of reasoning were followed consistently, the First Amendment, too, not just private property rights, would be undermined. All those newspapers and other publications sold in boxes standing on sidewalks could then be regulated by the government because they are also tied in with the public interest. They're sitting there in the street corner, right?

But, of course, you can't get away with that because the notion of freedom of the press and freedom of religion is particularly well entrenched in American culture and the press guards these vigilantly, even as many of its members champion government regulation of nearly everything else in society. So very few people dare to go up against the principle of freedom of speech, although, there are some who do it. For example, some feminists maintain that Hustler magazine, which hardly anyone disputes is a disgusting insult to women, should be shut down. They argue that contrary to widespread belief, pictures and words are like sticks and stones. In Canada, the Supreme Court accepted the idea! It agreed with Katherine MacKinnon, Professor of Law at the University of Michigan, who argued for it before that judicial body. She claimed that words can assault you, they're not, to use the title of the book she wrote on this topic, "only words" (McKinnon, 1996). But, in the American legal tradition anything which one can turn away from and ignore is not considered a case of assault. Yet even here there are some developments that are unsettling. Political correctness, especially at public education and work facilities, no longer gets firm legal protection from the courts.

Anyway, what these points aim to do is to raise the issue that in America we have a budding tradition of individual rights and sovereignty and in line with that tradition, the institution of taxation is an odd-ball, an anomaly, something strange. Just like slavery was, except slavery was a violation at a much more drastic, direct level. In a country that has declared that "all men are created equal" and that they have "unalienable rights", the exclusion of blacks was obscene, a direct contradiction.

But slavery wasn't the only contradiction to those ideas. Conscription, too, amounted to a partial enslavement of young people, for a cause that wasn't seen to be so abhorrent as slavery became. So it came under assault only in the mid-70s and eventually abolished in favor of a volunteer army, though not with unanimous welcome. (A while back the late Republican Senator Strom Thurmond of South Carolina issued a clarion call for it in the United States Air Force Academy's campus magazine! And after the 2006 Congressional elections Democrat Charles Rangel was doing the same!)

Clearly, national defense is a very important thing. And yet, it was recognized, at least by a decisive segment of the public, that to secure the defense of a country in a free society by conscripted labor is an anomaly. The point is that no matter how worthy the objective, the idea of a free society is that you have to persuade people to support it, no coerce them to do so.

Consider, again, the First Amendment—no matter how fervently religious leaders are convinced that all persons ought to believe as they do—be they Catholics, Methodists, Moonies or whatever— they don't get to coerce others to follow their faith. They must come to them with their persuasive skills and hope that they will agree to join up. They must gain consent from the potentially faithful. Once that consent has been gained, the practices that are demanded of the faithful are often harsh and certainly would not be tolerated if imposed by coercion.

Someone might respond to this by saying, well that's different. It should be a matter of personal choice, not of public policy, what people believe and how they worship and the practices they will adopt for themselves in the name of a religious creed. But consider, what could be more important than a belief or disbelief in God or eternal salvation? Very little.

Now if that has to be secured voluntarily, one would suppose that it would be fairly simple to realize, by the sheer logic of it, that anything else from citizens has to be secured voluntarily. The only case where force may be deployed is in response to force initiated by others, as in any case of self-defense. If somebody attacks you, you can pull out your mace, or your gun, or your karate chop and resist. Because the other started using force. But if one hasn't started to use violence or fraud against another, in a free society one may not be forcibly made to do anything.

In fact, that's behind the Fifth Amendment-Protection Against self-incrimination. One main reason that no one can be made to testify against himself is one is free at that point of a trial. The testimony would help prove something that needs to be proven before one may be coerced, namely, that one has done violence to another. But because one hasn't been proven to have violated any rights yet, one may not be coerced to testify. After conviction the matter changes because by one's violation of the rights of others, one has, in effect, asked to be penalized, such as locked up.

That is the best model for a legal system of a free republic, that only if one has violated other peoples' rights, may one be made to do things against one's will. Prior to that, it is forbidden.

However, the USA and other countries of the so called free world are far from having realized individual freedom consistently and completely. There are many anomalies left and taxation is one of them.

Now, is this critique correct? To decide there is a lot more to be done — for example one would have to argue with various theories of democracy and other forms of modern statism that seem relatively benign compared to massive totalitarian dictatorships and monarchical despotism.

Democracy's defenders claim, in essence, that when lots of people get together and decide that all of them must do something, then all of them must do it. Is this true? Is democracy a trump against individual rights? That's a very big issue. Arguments abound about the matter. (In support of the individualist stance, which I am taking here unabashedly, consider just a lynch mob. It has near universal agreement that someone ought to be hanged and yet, by violating the rights of the accused to due process of justice it is trumped, deemed unjustified.) Others argue that when people live in society, there is an implicit agreement that the democratic method trumps anything else, including individual rights.

Clearly, I have not gone through all those arguments. But I want to mention that there are quite a few and to deal with this topic fully would require more than I can do here. But my concern here is to indicate that there are feasible alternatives to taxation. I will discuss one of these.

Let me recall, first, that it is plausible enough that if individuals truly are to be in charge of their lives, they are the ones that ought to rule themselves, including the things that they've created, inherited or come by in other peaceful ways, ways that do not violate the rights of others. For example, Michael Jordan is very tall and agile, some of this due to his own determination, some of it due to his genetic make-up or early child rearing. But in a free country he gets to sell his assets, however peacefully he came by them, for a very large salary, right? Most of us are not as tall and not anywhere nearly as handsome as, say, Robert Redford and all the rest of those stars and celebrities in Hollywood, so we don't have this opportunity to sell our good looks to movies and magazines.

Mind you, some say that we have a right to what we deserve, but that is not the issue. Do I deserve my eye sight, my intelligence or my competence with languages? Does Bill Gates really deserve all his billions? Do you deserve that extra kidney you happen to have as part of your body?

No, these are not things that we and those who can sell what they have for a very high price necessarily deserve. It is a matter of what we came by peacefully, without violating the rights of others — be this the wealth others, most likely parents, have left us in their will, or a talent for playing the piano or some other attributes and assets other people are willing and eager to pay for so they may also utilize and enjoy.

If you have a right to your life, a right to your liberty, and a right to the pursuit of your happiness, then you may not be intruded upon by others no matter what. A sexually starved man may not rape, just because the woman is very appealing and desirable to him, even though she did not *deserve* having those attributes. She may even be an awful person, yet this has nothing to do with whether she has a right to have her sovereignty respected and may have it protected by herself, a body guard or a government.

So the question that needs to be asked here is what do we do if this theory is sound and thus taxation is precluded from society as a means for raising funds for government services because it violates our rights. How might a government of a bona fide, completely and uncompromisingly free society then be funded? How might a limited legal order, one that provides the most essential aspect of peace in a society, namely, the protection of everybody's rights, be financed?

I want to suggest an approach to understanding the nature of government as a bona fide public good that would undercut the problem associated with the provision of such public goods as national defense by the recognition that the provision of other, nonpublic (government provided) goods depends of providing the former, as well. Let me first sketch how this suggestion solves the problem of government financing.

The key to this idea is that a libertarian legal order or government would provide crucial yet unique private as well as public goods, and this would make it possible to secure the financing of government voluntarily. The provision of the private goods can be linked directly to the citizen-consumer, who would need to pay for it. Yet, given that the private good is a uniquely political good, providable only by or within the framework of a political/legal institution such as government, it would afford the opportunity to collect support for the public good that is also required. (Here the issue of anarchism arises, which I have dealt with elsewhere but simply want to fend off by noting that nothing about the idea of government being deployed here violates individual rights.)

Returning to the issue of rights protection as a public and private good, the protection of contracts is a private good that government provides at some level of the adjudicatory process in contractual disputes. Yet it has a public element, namely, due process. As the contract is upheld, no one's rights may be violated. Even if a dispute is handled by a private arbitration board, the government/legal framework must be there "in the wings" to assure due process in such matters as arrest, trial, imprisonment, and seizure of property, should the decision of the arbitrators be rejected by one of the parties.

The "national military defense" that government would provide is, of course, the classical public good. But government provides both these goods and payments for the former would also serve to fund the latter. In an imperfect analogy, this is similar to the way in which Coca Cola buyers pay for overhead and security provisions at bottling facilities even though, if asked to contribute money for these purposes, they might well refuse — on standard public goods grounds!

In spelling this proposal out a bit, let us first recall that the justification and need of government — or some facsimile — arises from the objective value to all members of society of living with others without personal military arming or ad hoc adjudication of disputes, and the general insecurity that goes with lawlessness. Individuals who recognize the value of social life readily acknowledge, in the spirit of the division of labor, the value of establishing an agency to provide them with the protection and preservation of their rights in the context of a system of objective law.[1]

Take contracts, for example. One of the benefits of social life is the possibility of extensive promise making for a variety of purposes — artistic, commercial, romantic, scientific, educational, recreational, athletic, and so forth. Sometimes relations among human beings are such that trust, danger of bad reputation, loss of friendship, etc., do not adequately assure against loss of value, against inadequate return on considerable investment, or against the perfor-

---

[1] Perhaps I should say that they *should* and probably will acknowledge the value of such an agency. This brings up the issue of how a government is properly established, something that comprises a crucial feature of the libertarian framework but is beyond the scope of the present essay. But see my "Human Rights, Feudalism, and Political Change", in Rosebaum (1980).

mance of outright victimization and injury. Some of these concerns can be handled by turning to insurance agencies. But sometimes, when matters are important and complex—and they very frequently are—satisfaction is obtainable only through legal protection, e.g., against the violation of human rights. Here, it is not simply some service, but some service aiming at justice, that is sought. Contracts are one way of insuring against serious loss and supporting efforts towards recovery, but by means that remain attentive to human dignity, that is, to the fact that no one is officially permitted to abridge the natural human rights of individuals in the community. Justly upholding the terms of contract is one government service. Government is the institution of a community specifically responsible for maintaining justice among members as members. This task is frequently accomplished only by the use of physical force, which government, by virtue of its unique adherence to the principle of due process—e.g., stringent rules of evidence, clear and present danger, probable cause, speedy and fair trial provisions, etc.—is established to carry out.

Promise breakers could have good reason for breaking their promises, but they would have even better reason to reassure their trading partners about the recovery of investment or avoidance of serious losses. Thus, even in usual utility-maximizing terms, members of society would ordinarily find it beneficial to secure the private good of government protection and enforcement of contracts (even if government is involved only as the ultimate protector—see the above discussion of arbitration). Especially in a human community in which traders do not know each other personally, then, the prospect of entering into enforceable contractual relationships is of considerable objective value to practically everyone.

For these and related reasons, it is plausible that the private good of having one's own liberty protected and preserved in the context of contractual relationships would be one of the most widely sought services of government in a free society. Every valid contract imposes a burden on the legal system and its administrators, for the "machinery" for interpreting and enforcing contracts, should disputes arise, must be in place. So providing this protection requires expenditures on the part of government. A system of contract fees, collected at the time if the signing or registering of contracts—from the most simple trades to elaborate corporate arrangements—with provisions for further payment in case of special services generated throughout the period of the contractual relationship, would provide funding for this government activity. Even the faintest appreciation for the staggering number of contracts drawn in contemporary societies within the span of just one day will suggest the revenue-obtaining potential of government work.

Like contract protection, other governmental services are deliverable to individuals, so fees for the services rendered could be established. Among such potentially individualized services are securing criminal justice and defending private homes and businesses or supervising such defense by private security agents so that due process of law is preserved.[2] Not only would it be possible to require payment for particular services rendered, but, if criminal actions are involved, burdens could be distributed in line with the determination of legal responsibility. For example, court costs could be imposed on guilty parties, and criminals could be required to cover other costs, such as police services.

For government to be able to carry out these functions, however — to stand ready for purposes of adjudicating disputes, defending persons and property, issuing warrants for arrest, seeking reparations, imposing penalties or imprisonment — it must be stable and secure. Government, in other words, has overhead costs, including those associated with providing for the defense of the system of laws itself. Foreign aggression, usually aimed at the country as a whole, is obviously a threat to this system. Once a country has been conquered, the foreigners take over the administration of justice and, with appropriate alterations (though by no means with even very dramatic ones), continue on the business of state, good or ill. Against this eventuality a government should protect the community, including itself — or, the institution of government must be so constituted that its protection of its own functions is provided for as a necessary means towards its provision of the protection and preservation of the rights of its citizens. Accordingly, its charges for the provision of its various services would reasonably include some amount to cover the cost of defense against foreign aggression. In this respect, the situation would be much like Coca Cola paying for security guards and other overhead costs from earnings from the sale of such clearly individually consumed goods as bottles of Coke.

---

[2] In some cases, the possibility of differentiating in service delivery may depend on technological developments, although it is more likely that it would simply require people's willingness to modify standard commercial practices to the services in question. Skeptics may wish to check out the method of customer differentiation devised by a private provider of fire protection. See Poole (1976), pp. 6–11.

It might be thought that in this way the principles of a free society, as conceived along libertarian lines, would be breached. First, would not everyone be required to pay for services? Second, would not those who might wish to compete in the provision of government's services be forcibly excluded?

Regarding the fear of reintroducing coercive financing, it must be observed that entering into contractual agreements, for example, is an entirely voluntary matter. Anyone can, literally, simply accept a handshake or friendly wink and not bother with contracts, just as one can avoid marriage vows and simply leave it at being lovers. Yet the existence of a legal system makes possible the legal protection of relations beyond the state of promises, should one desire this firmer protection. And such private goods, obtainable from government, would reasonably carry the burden of supporting the public good of national defense.

But what about the objection that in a free society government could not legitimately bar others from providing, say, contract protection. And then those others could offer it at a lower price, not having the national-defense overhead costs to worry about. So government would lose its private-goods customers, and this would still leave us with the public goods problem.[3]

This objection, usually advanced by economists with an anarchist libertarian viewpoint, can be met by noting that government is the political institution which is established and authorized to pursue justice in the social realm, making it a monopoly both in the sense of classical natural monopolies and in the sense of the requirement for internal integrity in the administration of justice. That is, on the one hand, the same services provided outside the legal framework would not be as valuable without provisions of due process of law. On the other hand, the ethical justification of establishing government implies that in human relations, where disputes often arise and sometimes culminate in conflict, an institution be invoked which is capable of providing for the most peaceful, least rights-violating procedures required for problem solving. In short, there will very likely be greater demand for government-backed arbitration proceedings, and the very logic of establishing government (from the ethical point of view of why they *should* be established) would generate this demand (see Machan, 1975).

Outside the context of a libertarian conception of government, this solution might be challenged on grounds, among others, that gov-

---

[3]   See, e.g., Friedman (1973), chapter 34.

ernmental costs are enormous and the very existence of deficit spending in most modern societies indicates that not even taxation can secure enough funding for government. In libertarian theory, however, the scope of government is severely confined to securing the protection and preservation of Lockean natural (individual human) rights. That is, only protecting and preserving everyone's Lockean rights are legitimate governmental concerns.[4] Although such a service is a public good that can be made private in its particular delivery (as detailed earlier), it is still a public good in the sense of its provision being good for members of the community as such, for citizens as citizens. But because there is a definite constraint on what constitutes such a public good, it should be plausible, at least, that its provision will not involve so much cost as is now commonly associated with governmental operations that range from some bona fide public goods — e.g., criminal law and national defense — to such nonpublic goods as national public radio, mail service, and the printing of money.[5]

In short, then, competition in providing legal protection and adjudication of contracts would be impossible because this good is not solely an economic but also a political good, the provision of which requires the existence and maintenance of an integrated legal system, including national defense.[6] To prohibit the provision of this good apart from the legal system is tantamount to prohibiting vigilante groups, lynching, and similar paralegal processes which always involve third parties whose rights are seriously endangered without the full protection of due process of law.

The fee-for-services-plus-overhead solution is not the only one that could be invoked to finance the administration of governments in a free society. As Ayn Rand (1973) has suggested, emergency funds could be raised through lotteries or by appealing for contribu-

---

[4] For the view that libertarian natural rights are not the familiar Lockean rights which impose only negative duties on others — e.g., the obligation to refrain form initiating physical force against others — but that they instead "involve providing people with positive benefit", see Nickel (1978–79). But this view is mistaken, and the mistake stems from the belief that human rights are rights against government as distinct from rights that should be respected by all and for the protection and preservation of which governments should be established. See my "Wronging Rights" (1981).

[5] I develop the argument for this in "Rational Choice and Public Affairs" (1980).

[6] For more on this see Kelley (1974). None of this precludes the free operations of security services, arbitration groups, etc., which are ultimately accountable to government and do not undertake the enforcement of decisions independently of government.

tions, e.g., in a time of war. The integrity of the system would be evident all along, so a genuine threat to the system requiring military
action could be demonstrated readily in public debate conducted by
a free press, the educational and scientific communities, and so
forth. When it is recalled that liberal democratic regimes are closest
to the policy envisioned by libertarians (and they have all along
received relatively solid popular support) the probability of support
for the libertarian system—including extraordinary support in
times of trouble—may also be assumed. But what is crucial is something else, namely, that it is not inherently impossible to secure the
public good of the maintenance of justice, including the protection
and preservation of the rights of citizens from domestic and foreign
aggression, without disregarding those very values.

There is, of course, no guarantee that a government of a libertarian
society *would be* voluntarily financed. Spells of neglect could settle
in, or there could be periods during which government is not
needed, when the world of the anarchist libertarian might be realized, at least for a brief period.[7] Yet, whenever the challenge is posed
to provide such a guarantee, it must be noted that coercive funding
of government is anything but a guarantee against governments'
going bankrupt, waging unsuccessful and unwarranted wars,
neglecting various related obligations, etc. Richard Tuck observes:

> It has been customary for political theorists to accept that [the
> free rider-public goods] argument is a good one, and to direct
> their energies toward devising strategies to cope with it. The
> most popular has undoubtedly been some mechanism of social
> coercion, despite the fact that such mechanisms characteristi-
> cally depend on cooperative action by the people concerned, and
> that the argument is therefore likely to turn into a *regressus ad
> infinitum.* ((Tuck [1977], pp. 147–48.)

If the false and impossible ideal of guaranteed provision of public
goods is rejected, as it should be, then the solution offered along lines
sketched above will have to be assessed comparatively.[8] It will have
to be judged in accordance with how well it would secure for members of human communities the values they should seek from a legal

[7]   Certain periods of individualist anarchism have occurred throughout
       human history. See, for an example, Peden (1977).
[8]   Further details and refinements of this and related tasks of a libertarian
       political system are, of course, required but it is usual for those to emerge
       only after the basic framework proposed is deemed workable. The political
       science and legal elaboration of libertarianism presuppose the basic
       plausibility of the general system.

system, granting that all such proposals carry risks of abuse and neglect, risks the elimination of which from human affairs is not only impossible but dangerous to pursue.

It is clear, I believe, that along these lines it is possible to bring the funding of government or legal administration of a free society in harmony with its basic principles of individual rights. This does not clinch the case against taxation, of course, since it hasn't been demonstrated beyond a reasonable doubt that persons do have such basic rights the violation of which ought to be uniformly and universally prohibited and resisted. But it does show that if that idea is sound, taxation must be given up in favor of another policy.[9] And the one here being suggested seems to be promising, at least.

---

[9] Which lies at the foundation of not just the American polity but many of the ideas that have captured the hearts and minds of people throughout the world concerning how government ought to be administered (i.e., respectful of human rights, admittedly loosely understood).

Chapter VI

The Ethics of
Private Property?

Let me begin by explaining what I mean by the right to private property and why I use what some consider now an old-fashioned term,
abandoned in favor of, say "the right to several property".[1] This right
is the social-political principle that adult human beings may not be
prohibited or prevented by anyone from acquiring, holding and trading (with willing parties) valued items not already owned by others.
Such a right is, thus, unalienable[2] and, if in fact justified, is supposed
to enjoy respect and legal protection in a just human community.

In the development of classical liberalism there emerged in Western political thought a shift of focus as to the prime value in
social-political matters, from the group—a tribe, class, state or
nation—to the human individual. It started with the effort to gradu-
ally transfer power from a few or even one person as the source of
collective authority and power to more segments of society involved
in exercising such authority and power, leading, eventually, to the
sovereignty of the human individual. The way in which power is dif-
fused when individuals are sovereigns rather than groups is
through the fact that individuals have only a little and highly diver-
sified power to wield. In consequences, they aren't likely to impose
themselves on others by, say, starting a war, even when they disagree very seriously. That, in essence, was one of the initial motiva-

[1] See, for example, Barnett (1998). One reason that it is useful, at least in the
     context of political philosophy and moral theory, to keep with the
     terminology of "the right to private property" is that this right is tied to an
     important element of classic liberal social and political thought, namely,
     individualism.
[2] While the right to own may be unalienable, what one owns isn't and may be
     traded, given away and even destroyed (as Karl Marx was so eager to point
     out in his essay "On The Jewish Question", in Marx [1977]).

tions for moving toward individualism, which, when implemented via law and public policy, is much more conducive to peace and, as a result, to prosperity than is any form of collectivism. The liberal order gained support, also, from the conflict between church and state, of course. Indirectly, however, here, too, intending to decentralize power was a major factor. The objective of becoming more productive via the invisible rather than visible hand also contributed to bolstering the case for classical liberal institutions.

Thus classical liberalism has had some considerable support on practical grounds — its usefulness to attaining various widely sought-after objectives. But one may ask, why would these practical consequences flow from establishing liberal institutions. Why is it better to have a more decentralized polity, an unplanned economy? Why would prosperity come more readily from the invisible rather than the visible hand?

Arguably the answer is that individualism makes better sense than its competitors because the view that *human beings are primarily parts of a social whole* is wrong. This last is a false notion. When invoked, it tends to serve as a disguise for certain special or vested privileges of some members of society.[3] Generalizing such special or vested interests, the values or goals pursued in their name, has been a major source of political acrimony throughout human history. It even continues to drive much of contemporary democratic politics.

There is, however, the problem that as far as its ethical presuppositions and implications are concerned, individualism and in consequence also classical liberalism have not fared all that well. These views are constantly being charged with opposition to community life and human fellowship, hedonism, materialism, and so forth. Even though this is wrongheaded, without a solid moral case it is difficult to show that to be true. The reason is that morality is extremely important in human affairs. Most people do not confidently embrace a political stance unless it manages to embrace cer-

---

[3]   This is what public choice theory, within contemporary political economy, has helped identify. See, however, Kincaid (1996), in which the author argues that the individualist stance in modern economics is mistaken and that we ought to deploy a more holistic approach. Kincaid and many other critics of what they dub "liberal individualism" claim that individualism is atomistic. While some may, certainly not all individualist fit this description. Nor is that the only version of individualism that gives rise to liberal politics. A good case in point is John Locke, among the early liberals, and many others such as Ayn Rand, Eric Mack, Douglas B. Rasmussen, Douglas J. Den Uyl, Fred D. Miller, Jr., and the late David L. Norton, in our own age.

tain basic moral principles. Pragmatic reasons thus never suffice to establish the soundness of political systems and public policies.

It is part of the point of this chapter to show that private property rights accord with certain basic moral principles. These are the indispensability of human agency in any sensible moral framework and the moral virtue of prudence. I will argue that individualism embraces these principles and that the right to private property makes their actual realization possible in human community life.

So here the question is "What is morally right about the institution of private property rights, why it is justifiable to have such laws in a community?" And by this I mean not to focus on such instrumental or pragmatic matters as how useful property law is for purposes of facilitating productivity or wealth or innovation. It may be all that, of course. Yet this chapter focuses on the even more crucial issue of whether that institution makes morally good sense or whether critics such as Marx are right to condemn it as a promoter of hedonism, selfishness and greed.

To go about my task with some hope of success I need to begin by saying something about the nature of morality. Basically morality concerns how to live one's life properly, rightly, in a worthy manner, nobly, honorably. To be morally good is to choose to do what will make a person excellent as the kind of being he is, to make one a human being who lives virtuously—honestly, prudently, generously, courageously and so forth.

To live a morally good life amounts to choosing to live so as to fulfill the requirements of one's nature. So our first task will be to take a brief glance at human nature.

Morality, Humanity and Individuality

Since Aristotle spelled it out explicitly, it has been clear enough and difficult to dispute that what makes us all distinctively human is that we have a self-awareness that consists of thinking, of understanding in concepts, and of guiding our conduct by principles not just spur-of-the moment feelings, wishes or desires. This is so widely evident in human life and history that, while philosophers like to discuss the nuances, no one can reasonably doubt it. What is less widely acknowledged is that human nature includes, as one of its distinctive features, a significant element of individuality. This is vital because private property rights ties in very closely with human individuality.

A quick indicator of this fact is the thought experiment in which one imagines that if a good friend dies, it is plainly nonsense to believe, "Oh well, I'll just replace my friend with someone else." One cannot just replace a person with another if one regards him as he is most basically, not just as some member of a class of people, such as dentists or auto mechanics. (Even with pets it's difficult to replace them because they become sort of humanized around us.)

On the other hand, with a cow, fly, rock and most other things in the world, replacing them is no problem in one sense because they aren't important *individually*. They're important in their relationship to other things, whereas in the case of human beings it is everyone's individuality that matters most, especially in those most significant personal or intimate relationships. You fall in love with an individual, not a banker — when you really fall in love, that is. (Some people "fall in love" with a type, true enough, but there's something perverse about that — it is somewhat sad to hear, "Well, I love him because he's in uniform or has a big car.")

Even apart from such common sense observations there is the clear evidence that whenever we consider human beings, we cannot avoid their volitional conduct, actions they choose to bring about on their own.[4] In intellectual discussions this is evident in the fact that we criticize one another about what we think, holding our adversaries directly or indirectly responsible for alleged misjudgments.[5]

It is a reasonable view, then, that human beings are first and foremost individuals who cause much of what they do. Their actions flow from their thinking and their thinking is the sphere in which they are free, self-determined.[6]

Individualism: True and False

Now individualism is associated somewhat uncomfortably with classical liberalism. The reason is that some have overemphasized the element of individuality, making it seem that we are not also members of communities, even of the human race. Such "atomistic" individualism has made it seem that classical liberalism is tied to a misguided social philosophy. An example of it may be found in the

[4]   Exceptions are individuals crucially incapacitated. Political theory and law are not devices for dealing with exceptions, however.

[5]   I develop much of this throughout Machan (1998a), especially in Chapter 13. "Individualism and Political Dialogue." Any kind of professional, including scholarly and intellectual, malpractice alleged in the course of political or other disputes implicitly rests responsibility with the interlocutors, blaming or commanding them for what they ought to or ought not to have done or said.

[6]   For more on this, see Pols (1982) and Machan (2000).

oft repeated story, by economists, of Robinson Crusoe. If one models human life on Crusoe's story and his interaction with Friday, it appears that we are born capable of self-sufficient productive conduct and from the start choose whether to associate with others. Yet this idea is patently absurd, considering that all human beings are born helpless and grow up in the company of others on whose support they vitally depend.

Yet it is not true that individualism is necessarily committed to atomism. One can fully admit to the communal aspects of human life while insisting that we are essentially individuals, as well. Such a robust, what I have called "classical" individualism, also stresses the importance of the private realm and insists that all bona fide human communities must adhere to the terms individuals set for themselves.

The crucial individualist ingredient of classical liberal social and political theory stresses not some arid independence or isolation of the individual human being but the fact that everyone can make what in principle can be independent judgments as to the kind of communities suitable to one's membership. Given human nature, the element of choice must be preserved in every suitable human community. This is the source of the classical liberal political principles that demands that the consent of the governed be upheld in public policy as well as personal relations. The criminal nature of murder, assault, kidnapping, rape, robbery, burglary and so forth all make sense in terms of this classical or moderate individualism first found in Aristotle's philosophy.[7]

Individuality and Privacy

The gist of individualism is, then, that everyone must consent to being used by another. This is because each is important, valuable in his or her own right. And if an individual is important as such, then

---

[7]   "To [Aristotle] the Individual is the primary reality, and has the first claim to recognition. In his metaphysics individual things are regarded, not as the mere shadows of the idea, but as independent realities; universal conceptions not as independent substances but as the expression for the common peculiarity of a number of individuals. Similarly in his moral philosophy he transfers the ultimate end of human action and social institutions from the State to the individual, and looks for its attainment in his free self-development. The highest aim of the State consists in the happiness of its citizens." Zeller (1897), pp. 224–26. This idea is developed further in Miller (1995). The difference between the atomistic and classical type of individualism is discussed in Machan (1990).

there is a sphere that constitutes the individual's realm of sovereignty and others ought to respect it, the realm within which one must make effective judgments about one's life. And indeed in classical liberal, political, and legal theory there's a great deal of emphasis on individual rights rather than rights of families or other groups, bearing on this individualist element of the position. The right to private property is, in turn, the most practically relevant of those individual rights.

The term "privacy", then, underlines this emphasis of the importance of individuals. The right to private property is really just an extension, within the framework of a naturalist world view, of the right to one's own life. It is when one('s life) engages with the rest of the world in the unique way one will do so, and when another will do this in his or her unique way, then privacy becomes important.[8] It will then be possible to actualize and to protect who one is and one's manifestation in the world — one's own art, productivity, creativity, innovation and so forth. None of those, as well, may be used by others without the individual's consent to whom they belong.

Socialism and Humanity

Now consider that one of the interesting things about socialism is that in deep-seeded socialist theory there are no individuals. Marx said it directly: "The human essence is the true collectivity of man." (Marx [1977], p. 126.) He also noted that human beings constitute specie-beings and comprise "an organic whole" in the collectivity we call humanity (Marx [1971], p. 39). What is important about you and me for a consistent, thoroughgoing socialist is that we belong to the human race, somewhat analogously to the way a bee belongs to

---

[8]   A very important beginning had been made on this line of analysis by William of Ockham who regarded property rights as securing "the power of rights reason", that is, a sphere of personal jurisdiction that made reasoning about what one ought to do possible. This was extended more elaborate in John Locke's idea that one has the right to one's person and estate, something that, if protected, makes choice among other persons possible. An even greater advance on the precise identification of the nature of private property had been made in James Sadowsky, "Private Property and Collective Ownership", in Machan (1974). Karl Marx, too, got it nearly right when he wrote that "the right of man to property is the right to enjoy his possessions and dispose of the same arbitrarily without regard for other men, independently, from society, the right of selfishness." Karl Marx, "On The Jewish Question", in Trucker (1978), p. 26. Only, Marx's warped view of human nature prompted him to consider only the most wasteful and pointless way the right to private property might be exercised.

its hive or an ant to its colony, only in this case the constituent parts are intelligent persons.

This is especially true of international socialism, but National Socialism and even more restrictive, local forms of socialism, emphasize the group as a whole and its plan, telos or destiny. Even communitarians, as vague as their conception of a community comes to (so that one cannot pin them down as socialists because they leave room for some elements of individualism), speak mostly of concerns in behalf of "us" and use the term "we" to designate the primarily valued party when discussing public policy. The individual can then, at times, be sacrificed if some gains are made for the group, collective or community.

Classical Liberalism, Human Nature & Individuality

Yet, if we examine human life carefully, we notice clearly that there is something irreducibly, inescapably, individual about everybody. Just think about yourself. How do you insist on being regarded by friends and others close to you? As a student? An American or Rumanian or Hispanic? Or as a woman or basketball player? Is there not in fact something unique that is the you that captures who you are? One's identity isn't racial, ethnic, religious or even professional. It is individual. As John Quincy Adams said in the motion picture *Amistad*, ask not what someone is but who someone is to come to know the person.

It's in classical liberalism that this is acknowledged more than in any other political philosophy. There's always been a little bit of emphasis on individuality, of course, in various rebellious political movements, but it's very difficult to maintain the supremacy of the tribe or, later, the state if one admits that what is truly important in a human society is the individuals who comprise it, as individuals. Because then one can't reasonably say, "Well, we can do away with that individual or with that group of individuals or their projects so as to benefit some others, including some collective such as the state, community, culture or race."

Indeed, with the recognition and acknowledgment of the supreme value of the individual, the very definition of a "good" or "just" society would have to emphasize the freedom and happiness of individuals.

In fact, a characteristic of the classical liberal political ethos is that one scrutinizes a society for its quality, its goodness, and its justice on the basis of how loyal it is to the mission of securing the rights of individuals to their liberty and pursuit of happiness. This is actually a very prominent movement in the world today. It's not done consistently and purely, but all those human rights organizations that go from country to country to check whether they adhere to tenets of justice are at least rhetorically committed to the examination of whether the legal authorities treat human beings who live in their jurisdiction as individuals who have basic rights. Are their projects respected or are they neglected and treated with callous disregard for their individual choices?

This is one of the reasons that in a largely liberal — or, for the sake of avoiding confusion with American liberalism, a libertarian — society membership in a class loses its moral and political significance. In the United States of American, for example there are matters that may make no difference to most people, but when they matter to even just one, it is appreciated. I, for one, once worked as a busboy in Cleveland, Ohio, and noticed that when paid, I could go back to the same restaurant and eat a meal there. There was no frowning and shaking of the head and saying, "Wait a minute, you don't belong here." In much of Europe, in contrast, if you work in a restaurant you don't get to eat there — it is not illegal now but it's certainly gauche.

Fluctuating Classes

In a more or less libertarian social-political society the divisions that are based on incidental attributes — one's wealth, color, national origin, ethnicity, race, and so forth — tend to be less significant because one's individual worth trumps all these and classes, at any rate, are always in a flux. Even racial and ethnic, not to mention religious or economic categories tend to shift because there is no widespread and well entrenched legally enforced barriers to either entry to or exit from any of them.

Such categories and the behavior associated with them may still prevail in certain special contexts. For example, a professor will usually attain special respect in the classroom, but when one meets the professor at a restaurant, one will not need to carry over the behavior associated with that classroom status. No "Herr Doctor", as, for example, in much of Germany, in or outside the classroom. In most American schools, however, one says, "Hello Professor", but outside the label isn't usually used.

All this can be a bit disturbing because it can sometimes spill over into disrespect for people who in fact deserve respect. Rampant individualism can corrupt into disrespect for all authority. The corruption can but by no means need be generated by the notion that individuals matter primarily as individuals, not so much as members of classes. It is also evident enough that we are social beings, members of the class of human beings, and there are some matters very important about that, too.

The Moral Standing of Private Property Rights

Individualism does, however, underlie the regime of private property rights. But why do we need a separate discussion of the merits of the right to private property? What will such an inquiry yield?

There are at least two answers to that question. One is that when you resist people taking something from you, by taxation, theft or any other means, it is important to know, even if only implicitly, that the resistance is justified. That it is a kind of self-defense, akin to resisting someone assaulting or raping someone else. It is vital to learn that one is in the right and is not doing something merely willful or stubborn or prejudicial, that one is not just being a recalcitrant, antisocial person, when one insists on the integrity of ownership. This is a point widely contested by opponents of classical liberal or libertarian legal orders.

When all things are considered, the most important questions about liberalism and its various tenants is, "Is it true?" "Is classical liberalism or, its purest versions, libertarianism, the way a society ought to be organized?" And, in order to answer that question, one must examine whether its various tenets can withstand challenges, criticisms and so on. Individualism is one of these tenets but the right to private property is the most important practical, public policy element of it.

The second reason we need to examine private property rights is whether system of individual rights, including the right to private property, is a just system? Or is it, as many critics claim, just a figment of some people's imagination?

One of the most prominent and oft-repeated criticisms leveled at classical liberalism, especially by students of various configurations of Marxism — there are about 300 versions now — is that this whole emphasis on individuality is a kind of a historical glitch. It's only a temporary phase in history which had its role but now can be dispensed with.

Individualism and Historicism

The Marxists and many others, some who follow them without knowing it, claim that in the 16th century the individual was invented, not merely discovered or his existence politically affirmed, for the sake of sustaining economic productivity. In order to create motivation for wealth-creation, the individual had to be made seem significant. It's a myth, but it's a useful myth. It's like telling someone that she is beautiful when she isn't so that she will do certain things from which certain advantages derive. According to Marxists, there was a period of human history where the belief in the importance of the individual had an objective historical function, not because it's true, but because it contributes to certain crucial elements of capitalism.

There are people who look at history in this way, as if it is the record of the growth of humanity from infancy to full maturity. They then take it that the bourgeois epoch is like the adolescence of an individual. It's a temporary stage and has its usefulness because, typically, adolescents embark upon all sorts of useless ventures — such as getting up at four o'clock to drive someplace, not because there's something important to do, but as a sort of exercise to prepare for adulthood. It trains them for the eventual serious challenges of maturity.

When one treats humanity this way, so that it has these various historical stages, individualism can be regarded to be one of those stages. It's a somewhat appealing picture — it fits some images we have of humankind. Ecologists encourage this, as do some moral visionaries who see humanity as a big family or some other kind of collectivity.

Marx explicitly said that the Greek era was the childhood of humanity. He, as I have noted already, and many of those who have been influenced by his thinking believe that humanity is some kind of organism, a being of which individuals are the parts. Humanity goes through stages of organic development, the tribalism its first and communism its final stage. And while the individualist stage in a necessary one, it is certainly not the completed stage of humanity.

Individualist Alternative to Organicism

These challenges have to be answered because they are extremely well developed, plausible enough, and with enormous influence in the world intellectual community. It is a little like when one meets a friend and asks them to explain some event such as their recent divorce and they proceed to give you a very well worked out and sincerely held rationalization as to how things happened. Now, in order to cope with one of these rationalizations, one must get to the heart of the actual situation and demonstrate beyond all reasonable doubt that the story is a different one. One must show that one's understanding of what's going on is more rational, coherent, comprehensive, and explains much more than does theirs. Otherwise the deceptive story will be the only viable account making the rounds, despite its conflict with common sense.

Unless liberalism is able to identify a better story than what those who champion the organic view advance, it will be defeated, at least theoretically. And while that isn't always decisive, it certainly has an impact on the confidence with which the position can be supported and implemented.

Indeed, one of the advantages of anti-liberal doctrines is that so many intellectuals are enchanted by them. They create elaborate and smart stories around them, stories that are extremely appealing and intellectually challenging. For one, such a story gives the intellectual a privileged position. Only intellectuals are in the position to grasp such a complex story, after all. Common sense does not support it. (For example, Marx thought only communists could really understand the truth of such a story, the rest of us having been blinded by our class outlook.)

The Appeal of Collectivism

The idea, for example, that we are all mere parts of a large human organism, humanity, has very a strong intellectual standing in our time. A great many people make reference to humanity — as when they talk about sacrificing oneself or one's private interests or one's materialistic goals for humanity. And others refer to smaller groups — the community or ethnic group or the race — as the organisms that are of significance.

So it's almost a feature of the mainstream to think of us not as individuals but as parts of some larger whole. "Don't you have something more important to live for than yourself?" "Isn't there something greater than yourself to which your life must be devoted for it to be worthwhile?" Less loosely, some, such as the philosopher Charles Taylor, argue that we all must *belong* to a group, by dint of our very humanity, our nature as human beings. He tells us that "Theories which assert the primacy of rights are those which take as the fundamental, or at least a fundamental, principle of their political theory the ascription of certain rights to individuals which deny the same status to a principle of belonging or obligation, that is a principle which states our obligation as men to belong to or sustain society, or a society of a certain type, or to obey authority or an authority of a certain type." (Taylor [1985], p. 188.) Never mind that Taylor cannot give us any such theories — John Locke, for example, rested basic human rights on ethics or natural law. What is important in what Taylor says is that if you just live to make the most of your life, you're not really living a *significant enough* life. A significant life must fulfill a greater purpose and humanity's purpose is one of the candidates. God's purpose is another candidate. Ecologists have a biological purpose in mind. But a significant life, by this account, one that belongs to the effort to pursue this purpose, may be *forcibly subordinated* to such purposes.[9]

There's a very prominent tradition of selecting alternative wholes larger than ourselves as the proposed beneficiaries of significant human actions. And this can lead to the whole process of forcing individuals to be used for purposes to which they do not consent. This is the greatest source of coercive thinking in human history. Once it is accepted that human individuals are part of a larger whole they, as members of a partnership or team, have enforceable obligations to the goals of that large whole. They belong to it.

Consider, to appreciate this, how in certain cases we treat such wholes as ourselves. If something happens to one's ear, for example, and yet one prizes one's appearance with an intact ear, then one takes another part of one's body that's not visible and takes part of it so as to replace the ear. The famous Welsh actor, Richard Harris, had his nose destroyed in a fight, so doctors took a part of his hip bone and replaced it, clearly because the nose was more important to an actor than that little part of the hip bone.

Well, if humanity is the larger organism, then maybe a given individual may not be so important a part of it as another. So the less important individual can be sacrificed for the more important one (or the goals of the less important can be sacrificed for those of the more important). One may be an eye and the other just a useless

---

[9] The concept "belong" can be used to refer to membership as well as to being a part of. Membership in human communities embarking on various purposes can be voluntary but being a part of is something ontologically pregnant — one is part of something sometimes whether one likes it or not. Taylor seems clearly to mean by "belong" "being part of", so that one can be compelled to adhere to the purpose at hand.

thumb. That picture is widely embraced because of the belief that humanity is some organic whole.

If one recognizes collectivism as a misguided picture of human life, one must carefully and effectively argue in response to these well worked out and often honestly and sincerely meant doctrines. One must demonstrate that it is indeed individuals who count for the most in the human picture. It needs to be proven, some of the widespread opinion to the contrary notwithstanding, that notions such as "individual rights" are universal and not stuck to some limited historical epoch.

The Right to Private Property

One reason that it must be shown that the social regulative principle of a right to private property is sound and that it ought to be respected and protected in human community life is that it is a vital conceptual or logical implication of the individualist story. If individualism is indeed sound, so is the principle of private property rights. When the right to private property is not respected and not sufficiently protected, then there is something wrong with a community.

This means that it is not quite fit for human inhabitation, given the individuality of every person and how respect for this is a precondition for his or her flourishing.

There are many different ways in which private property has been supported in the history of political economy. Most prominent has been the claim that there should be legal protection of the right private property because this facilitates productivity — a point that's in agreement with Marx, only universalized beyond a given epoch. Protecting this right helps society get rich — not only in the 16th century but always. Both Adam Smith and John Stuart Mill tended to argue along these lines: It's a good thing to have these rights because if we act in terms of them we will have greater prosperity. Many economists today argue a similar point. Indeed, that is one reason many governments engage in privatization, so as to encourage economic growth.

All of this is vital but it isn't what is most important. What needs to be shown is that the individual has these rights regardless of what's done when simply exercising them. Even if individuals waste away their lives, they have that right. It is theirs to waste away, not someone else's, because they are the important element of society, not some outsider, not some other being such as society, the community, the tribe or the ethnic group. It is this element of liberty, the right to choose how one lives, that is most central to human community life, even if, indeed because, as a matter of one's personal life it is equally important to make the right choice, to choose to do the right thing.

That is exactly why the right to private property is vital. When effectively protected, it secures for human individuals a sphere of personal jurisdiction, the right to acquire and hold the props, as it where, with which to order one's life. Moral virtues such as generosity, kindness, courage, moderation, prudence and the rest are all imperatives the practice of which engage one with the natural world. If one is not in charge of some of that world, at least oneself, one cannot conduct oneself virtuously. So the right to one's life, liberty and property are necessary conditions for a morally significant or meaningful life in human communities.

It needs to be noted here, as a significant aside, that even if we are essentially individuals, this doesn't mean we are not also naturally members of societies. But, as moral agents and as candidates for membership in some human communities or societies, we are morally responsible to take into consideration and never neglect the fact that we must judge those societies as to whether they do adequate justice to our individuality, most generally, and whether they best serve our flourishing.

No *Carte Blanche* to Communities

From this it follows that we must always keep in focus the question of whether we ought to live in a given community. Do we — ought we to — want to support this kind of public policy, this kind of a legal system? What is the standard by which we make that kind of decision when we have the chance? At the most basic level of community concern must lie the issue of what principles should govern human communities. The right to private property is one of those principles.

Very often we don't have a direct practical option to act on the choice we make about basic principles. But at least we can think about them so that when we do get a chance to make a significant decision, then we will know where to stand. We owe it to ourselves, to a life of integrity, not to forget about that issue, ever. That is the highest duty of citizenship!

Property Rights, Individuality and the Moral Life

So what does the right to private property do in connection with the essential human element of individuality?

Well, as already suggested, the right to private property secures for one a sphere of sovereignty. See, if we are individuals, required, morally, to lead our lives by our judgements, it is crucial that we control the elements with which our lives are lived. Indeed, it becomes the most crucial thing.

The question, "How ought I to live?" becomes the foremost question to which you then seek an answer. While we aren't moral theoreticians and ethical philosophers and so on, that question still is always near the forefront of our minds. No matter what you do, even reading these lines, the question will arise: "Should I sleep or should I pay attention? Should I consider this point or should I just glide over it?"

All of those are questions having to do with your ethical agency, with one's governance of one's life, with one's sovereignty. One's feeling that one is doing the right thing becomes crucial if one is indeed the master of one's existence.

Now, without the right to private property, without having some props, some elements of reality that are under our jurisdiction, our ethical decisions cannot be effectual. Consider for example, if it turns out to be true that a good human being ought to be generous. Well, if we do not have the right to private property how are we going to be generous? Are we going to be like politicians and bureaucrats and expropriate what belongs to others and give this to the poor and needy? That's not generosity. That's theft.

In short, then, in order to have a effective life of moral virtue, for example the virtue of generosity, we must have the right to property, to hold and then to be free to part with values, on your own terms.

Moral Individualism

Although collectivism has some currency, especially among intellectuals and social theorists, so does a particular version of individualism. I have in mind the sort that pertains to moral responsibility.

Few people ever quite let go of the idea that some things they and others do are good and some bad, and that those doing them are responsible. When others judge our lives, or when we reflect upon ours, we say, "I did or didn't do the right thing." Moreover, we can go on to consider what we did with what belongs to us — use it well or badly.

Without our sphere of sovereignty, that's manifest in the actual world where we live our lives, we would not be able to act on most moral principles, especially those that involve allocating resources.

Are we stingy? But one has to be stingy with something. If one is a neat person, one has to be neat within some sphere that one keeps orderly. If a slob, one will need something that belongs to one that one isn't taking good care of. If those items don't belong to you, if you always have to ask permission of society or the clan or the tribe or the nation as to what to do with these things, then you are not the effective agent in their disposition. And you are then not an effective moral agent either. You cannot take pride in what you achieve, nor feel guilt for your failings. You are basically just a little bit of a cell in this larger organism.

The Virtue of Prudence

Prudence is one of the virtues identified in classical Greece. I want now to discuss it in a little more detail than thus far.

First, in the modern era prudence has been demeaned because the task of taking care of oneself and one's own has been deemed to be instinctual ever since Thomas Hobbes argued that we are all driven to preserve ourselves. But Hobbes rested his case on extrapolating the principles of classical mechanistic physics to human life, a move that is not at all justified. Human beings must choose their conduct, including whether they will serve others' or their own well-being. Prudence, as the ancients saw it, is the virtue one needs to take decent care of oneself.

Later Immanuel Kant argued that since prudence is a motivation that is aligned to one's own interest or inclinations, it is not a moral virtue. Only motives that are totally indifferent as to one's own interest or inclinations can have moral significance, even though we can not know whether we are ever so purely motivated.

Neither Hobbes nor Kant had it right. Prudence is a moral virtue, though not the only or highest one. In any case, a prudent person acts, among other ways, economically. Such a person realizes that one must reserve for the future, put resources away for a rainy day. Such a person isn't reckless in the disposition of the resources over which he or she has control.

But now if we have no right to acquire or hold things then we can't be prudent. We then don't have the decision-making authority to allocate resources in accordance with standards of prudence. On the other hand, if we do have this authority, then we can choose to act prudently.

Prudence and Justice

If in fact it is a moral virtue to be prudent, but it's politically impossible for one to act on that virtue, then there is a basic conflict between ethics and politics. Then the political sphere is not properly *adjusted* to the ethical sphere. Then our ethical agency has not been done sufficient justice by the legal system in which we act.

And, indeed, that is one of the things that is so frustrating in societies where one does not have the right to private property. Not only that one is going to be thwarted in one's efforts to acquire life's necessities, but that one cannot act responsibly. Here what happens is a version of the tragedy of commons.

The tragedy of commons is a problem usually associated with managing the environment. The reason is that most spheres where there are environmental problems are public. The atmosphere, oceans, rivers, large forests and so on are spheres wherein no one is individually responsible. To put it another way, everyone is responsible for the management of such spheres but no one has a clear idea what to do about this responsibility because the limits imposed by private property rights are missing.

When you have a distinct or definite sphere of jurisdiction, however complicated it may be—with various layers of responsibility and delegation—then when something is done wrong, it can be traced to the agent or agents who did it. And when things are done right, again it can be traced to the agent or agents whose responsibility it was to do them right. Without the right to private property this is impossible.

This is one of the reasons that no society can completely abolish private property. It is impossible to act in any sort of responsible way without some sphere of personal jurisdiction.

Moral Responsibility and Private Property

So the right to private property is the concrete manifestation of the possibility of responsible conduct in a community where there are lots of people who need to know what they ought to do and with what they ought to do it. We are talking about a life lived within the context of the natural world. If our bodies are non-existent and we are just living in an illusionary material world, then these matters are of no significance. There is an assumption underlying the right to private property, and indeed many other elements of classical liberalism or libertarianism, namely, that we have a task to live properly in the midst of a natural environment, a natural world. We are not just living a purely immaterial life. Food needs to be grown and distributed, production has to occur. All sorts of concrete, natural tasks need to be carried out in order to facilitate our human lives.

If this natural life turns out to be either illusionary or insignificant, then some of these things loose their importance. Then politics might indeed be subject to different principles, ones that facilitate different goals, different aims from prosperity, flourishing, or other kinds of earthly success. It's not easy to imagine what that would be. Yet, in a philosophical discussion of these issues, one has to contend with the fact that there are alternative basic ideas that are proposed concerning the basic elements of human living. Liberalism has to stand the test of being compared with these alternative pictures.

Naturalism and Politics

The naturalist approach, in the sense we are preparing and forging ways of living within the natural world, is, I am convinced, demonstrably sound. The alternatives tend to be very vaguely and confusedly supported.

There are doctrines in the world that say that all individuality, for example, is a myth. There are Eastern religions that contend that the natural, individual self is an illusion and that in truth, we're all just part of the universal consciousness.

In order to test this, one has to have some criteria by which truth needs to be determined. The naturalist approach rests on the application of criteria that are universally accessible, available to all human beings with their rational faculties intact.

Commerce and Property

Private property rights, of course, sustains the institution of commerce. If you trade goods and services, if you sell them, if you produce them, if you hoard them, if you save them, you have to have some level of jurisdiction over them. If I wanted to trade you my watch for your shirt, then it has to be my watch. Or I have to have delegated to me the authority of someone whose watch it is. And it has to be your shirt; otherwise there would be no ability or justification in engaging in this trade. I can't sell you something that belongs to another. And if it belongs to everyone all at once, no one can sell or trade it and chaos prevails as regards to its use. So commerce, as well as charity and generosity presuppose the institution of private property rights. Without that institution, these activities cannot be under-taken smoothly, without confusion.

Moral Standing of Political-Economic Systems

One of the questions that arises in the discussion of political philoso-phy and political economy is whether they have moral standing. When the Left criticizes classical liberals morally because the liberal or libertarian polity makes profit-making possible, what is the answer?

It's not enough to just say, "Well, we just like to make profit." A murderer can just say, "We just like to kill people." That is no justification, clearly.

There are those who argue that a social science such as economics requires nothing from morality—indeed, it is entirely amoral, purely positive or descriptive in its central thrust. But this is a mis-take. All human affairs, including economic ones, are permeated with moral issues. In economics, for example, there is the moral (or as Rasmussen and Den Uyl [1990] have called it, the meta-norma-tive) element of private property rights.

If one does not own anything, no trade can ensue and all the talk of supply and demand must be abandoned in favor of what collectivists tend to support, a sort of share-and-share alike "econ-omy." But to own something means to be in a distinctively norma-tive relationship with others. They are prohibited from taking what belongs to one. They ought not do so and will be penalized, further-more, if they do.

So the amoral stance on the market economy is doomed to failure. What is needed is a moral or other normative justification of the institution of private property rights.[10]

To do that we must analyze human nature as it is manifest in the natural world. Will such an analysis support the institutions of free-dom and free markets and give them a stronger moral standing in human society than alternative ones possess?

Morality and Public Affairs

Now there are some who would dismiss all this because there are cases in human community affairs involving innocent helpless per-sons, one's who meet with natural disaster and may find themselves without any voluntary help when they need it. And that is certain a possibility, even if not a likelihood in a free society. James Sterba, for

[10]   For more on this, see Machan (1998b), pp. 43–46.

example, has been arguing for decades that because such cases are possible, the people who find themselves in them have a right to welfare that the legal order may protect. These positive rights, whereby others are required to work for such persons — or part with goods they have worked for in order to support them — come about because it would not be reasonable, Sterba argues, to demand that such people respect private property rights. It would be more reasonable to expect of them to strive to obtain the goods they need — ones Sterba calls, in a question-begging fashion, surplus wealth. (As if someone is justified in identifying what constitutes surplus — a term from classical Marxism that makes no sense outside the Marxist framework.)

If one recognizes, however, that an individual's life is his or her own and he or she does not belong to anything or anyone outside of memberships to which he or she consents, then even the most dire needs of others does not support any institutional arrangement that fails to recognize individual rights — to life, liberty, and, yes, property (that one comes by without violating the rights of others even if one does not strictly deserve the property for some kind of service rendered or other achievement — for instance, come by because others want to purchase some talent or other attribute one naturally has). Just as it is unjustified to use others as a shield against natural danger, regardless of how little use one may make of them, one may not use others against their will, including wealth they own. One must find ways around this prohibition, as indeed most do when they engage in trade rather than theft in the effort to acquire their own wealth.

It is reasonable to demand this of everyone, even those in dire straits. If, however, in desperate circumstances such people do not honor this prohibition, there can be some measure of forgiveness, even within the purview of the legal authority (as per some cases that have been subject to unusual judicial discretion). But such exceptions, as hard cases in general, make bad general law.

Law and Common Sense

Let me go back to where we started. When somebody robs another who resists, the latter has a common sense idea of doing the right thing, that the resistance is not merely some immature, capricious and willful conduct. It is not as if one were simply engaged in footstomping and crying, "I want it! I want it! I want it!" No, one senses that there is right on one's side, not just an arbitrary wish and desire.

That is one reason it is vital to consider whether the free system can be given justification. What has been said here is by no means a thorough defense of the right to private property, but it does furnish some hints as to how such a defense would have to be presented if the issue ever arises, which is quite often in our world. First, this right, if protected, preserves one's moral agency in this natural world in which community life occurs. Furthermore, it punctuates the fact that striving to prosper is a morally valid goal for human beings. So, the moral virtue of prudence, of taking the requisite actions to care for oneself and one's intimates, supports the right to private property as well.

One thing that respect and protection of private property rights makes possible is the pursuit of wealth. Oddly, however, that is a *criticism* many offer against the system of free market capitalism that is built on the legal infrastructure of private property rights. They say, as we have already seen Marx do so, that private property rights—if they are protected, maintained, developed as law— encourage a hedonistic, narrowly selfish life, one that is concerned exclusively with acquisition of worldly goods. As he said, "the right of man to property is the … right of selfishness." Freedom is supposed to make too much self-indulgence, including pleasure, possible.

So another question that arises here turns out to be, "Is pleasure justified?" For even if the right to private property could be used for purposes quite different from obtaining pleasure in life, if pleasure is something loathsome and this right somehow encourages its relentless pursuit, perhaps it is an institution that is much more harmful than benign.

We cannot enter this topic at length but this much should suffice for now. If we are indeed natural beings in this world, one of our important values will be pleasure, the good feelings we experience *via* our bodies. This is so even if there are higher goods the attainment of which may require giving up some pleasure.

So, now, if wealth brings with it the possibility of pleasure, then wealth itself is a worthy good, provided it is not stolen but created, produced, and that it is not chosen as the highest good if a higher one can also be identified.

Abandon the Divided Self Idea

If one has a completely different view of human nature, whereby only the spiritual side of human life is of significance, then one will embrace a different system of values and probably also champion different institutions. We have a powerful tradition in most civilizations whereby there is an uneasiness about facilitating the flourishing of the human body. And that is often what stands, at a most basic level, against the free society!

One reason underlying that stand is the lack of a clear, unambiguous and benign acceptance of our earthly selves. We often think ourselves to be so unique, so extraordinary that we believe we must be partly divine or otherworldly. St. Augustine said it well when he cried out, "How great, my God, is this force of memory, how exceedingly great! It is like a vast and boundless subterranean shrine. ... Yet this is a faculty of my mind and belongs to my nature; nor can I myself grasp all that I am. Therefore the mind is not large enough to contain itself. But where can that uncontained part of it be?" (*Confessions*, Lib. X, ch. 17. 8ff.) And he then answered, as have millions of others, that it must be somewhere apart from nature.

Business, too, has a bad reputation because of this, as well as the free market place, because if our natural selves are somehow inferior, than servicing it with the vigor with which people in business do must be misguided. People who pursue profit or material wealth, would then be pursuing trivia. They would be mere hedonists. As the title of one of my articles put it, "Praise Mother Teresa and then Hit the Shopping Malls." In other words, we live a schizophrenic life. We embrace the value of prosperity, economic success, wealth on the one hand but then we deny it on the other.

Yet, if in our lives we embrace our bodies, minds, emotions, sensations and so on, then we suggest by this that a more integrated view of how to live and how to protect our values is right, not one that tears us into warring pieces.

The private property rights system rests, in part, on such an integrated understanding of human life, not the schizophrenic one. It rejects the idea that each human being is divided, a view that much of our literature embraces. It places us squarely on this earth, even though it is by no means hostile to anyone who chooses to look elsewhere for fulfillment, quite the contrary. (Indeed, the right to private property has made religious pursuits extremely fruitful as well as abundant, especially in the United States of America where churches can purchase their own land and welcome parishioners where they will not be disrupted by their foes.

The divided self idea started with Plato, at least with a certain reading of him, where he takes our minds to be divided from our bodies and where the mind is supposed to hold the rest of ourselves in check, rule it firmly. Major writers, especially theologians, have ever since stressed this drama and it is reflected in our society's institutions. Victor Hugo made note of this point:

> On the day when Christianity said to man: You are a duality, you are composed of two beings, one perishable, the other immortal, one carnal, the other ethereal, one enchained by appetites, needs, and passions, the other lofted on wings of enthusiasm and reverie, the former bending forever to earth, its mother, the latter soaring always toward heaven, its fatherland — on that day, the drama was created. Is it anything other, in fact, than this contrast on every day, this battle at every moment, between two opposing principles that are ever-present in life and that contend over man from the cradle to the grave? (Hugo, 1973)

Even secular thinkers, such as Adam Smith, tended to accept this dichotomization of two sides of the human self when he noted, in his famous remark, that "It is not from the benevolence of the butcher, the brewer, or the baker, that we expect our dinner, but from their regard to their own interest. We Address ourselves, not to their humanity but of their advantages."[11] Why juxtapose our humanity with our advantage? Aristotle and other ancients didn't when they accepted prudence as a *bona fide* moral virtue.

As a result of this popularization of our allegedly divided self, many of us are often apologetic when pursuing a satisfactory, happy life here on earth. And then we find it difficult if not impossible to defend the political regime that most clearly enhances such a life, becoming defensive when others maintain that, well, it is a mundane, materialist life that such a regime supports. Which is probably

---

[11] Adam Smith, *The Wealth of Nations* (1994), pp. 26–27. But see also Smith's observation, in this very same work, lamenting the very same point at issue here. Smith notes that "Ancient moral philosophy proposed to investigate wherein consisted the happiness and perfection of a man, considered not only as an individual, but as the member of a family, of a state, and of the great society of mankind. In that philosophy the duties of human life were treated of as subservient to the happiness and perfection of human life. But when moral, as well as natural philosophy, came to be taught only as subservient to theology, the duties of human life were treated of as chiefly subservient to the happiness of a life to come. In the ancient philosophy the perfection of virtue was represented as necessarily productive to the person who possessed it, of the most perfect happiness in this life. In the modern philosophy it was frequently represented as almost always inconsistent with any degree of happiness in this life, and heaven was to be earned by penance and mortification, not by the liberal, generous, and spirited conduct of a man. By far the most important of all the different branches of philosophy became in this manner by far the most corrupted."

responsible, more than anything else, for the unrelenting moral disdain exhibited in most cultures toward capitalism, even while as a practical matter the system simply cannot be dispensed with.

Mind you, there are many people with a dualistic bent — e.g., Acton, Cobden, Bright, Bastiat, and Tocqueville — who have favored the liberal political order. That is not at issue here. Argumentatively, however, they are not able to show the morally compelling merits of its capitalist order since they are bound to the view that the pursuits of this world are not so vital to human beings as the pursuits of a supernatural one. Prudence includes concern for economic prosperity as a priority only if the self whose well-being is to be looked after is largely the living, actual self of this world. If it is not, if the vital elements of the human self pertain to one's afterlife, then moral the imperative to seek to prosper in life can easily be undercut with the moral imperative to prepare for the after life. This preparation may indeed require foregoing — and has often been urged to supercede pursuing — the prosperity that is possible in this one.

The fact that dualism undermines the case for a free, capitalist, classical liberal order does not mean no dualists have supported one, only that this support has been vulnerable to criticism from within their own frame of reference. That alone is reason why the idea of the divided human self must be seriously rethought.[12] Without serious modification of it, based on the evidence of everyday lives and history, the best socioeconomic system human beings have ever identified will fail to gain moral standing and to flourish.

---

[12] This is not to say that everywhere the dualist conception of the human self is in vogue, quite the contrary. In most ordinary, practical contexts people think and talk in ways that shows clear awareness of the fact that we are multifaceted, multi-dimensional beings rather than ones consisting only of two irreconcilable elements, mind and body. That latter idea arises more out of theory than practice.

Chapter VII*

Justice and the Welfare State

Imagine someone who stole a composition from its creator and claimed it as his own. Surely, the fame and fortune which may result from this theft could not be considered justly acquired. Imagine, again, someone who has been bound and gagged in a chair in his home and misses an important appointment as a result, the consequences of which are disastrous. The blame, punishment, or related adverse result our victim suffers if people do not believe his story cannot justly be considered his due. A mere case of intentionally tripping another where the result can be a broken watch or a broken head suffered by the victim further shows that where agency cannot be established — where harm or advantage befalls someone other than the person who caused the injury or benefit — we cannot justly assign responsibility for consequences. Nor do we praise a student who passes an examination by copying the answers from another's paper.

The examples could continue. But what is their point? They serve, in this case, the purpose of an introduction to a discussion of political philosophy.

Take any political system in which it is impossible to determine who is responsible for the various events, situations, etc. that result from human action, one in which responsibility is misassigned or indeterminate because the laws and regulations which comprise the *legal* system of the *political* system render correct determination impossible — such a political system is in its most important respects *unjust*. While some elements of justice may be a *de facto* part of that society, as an organized institution the society is unjust. In this paper

* This paper was originally published in *The Personalist* (1970) and reprinted in Tibor R. Machan, *The Libertarian Alternative* (Chicago: Nelson-Hall, 1974).

I will show that ours is this kind of a society; i.e., I will show that the legal system we have, comprised of various laws (and regulations, backed by laws), make it impossible correctly to determine the responsibility for the consequences of the actions of citizens.

By examining any one of the examples listed earlier, it can be seen that the reason for the distortions in determining the responsibility for the events which ensued was that those who partook of the situation were either coerced or coercing others in some way — freedom of action was hampered. It is only if the coercion becomes evident, and the agent of the coercion is identified, that determination of responsibility can be made and the various situations can be treated justly. The thief gained fame and fortune by depriving the composer of his freedom to act (such as to sell or keep his composition). The bound and gagged victim was suffering consequences unduly when his failure to attend the meeting in question had adverse consequences for him (and others). The man who was tripped was deprived of his freedom to act as well, while the chap who copied the answers from his schoolmate reaped unearned grades, both cases being paradigms of injustice. In all these examples the central feature is — with varying degrees of complexity — that one man deprived another of his freedom to act as he could have chosen.

On a socio-political scale the situation is markedly similar. Slavery, to take a rather drastic example, makes it impossible to determine who is responsible for consequences of the slave and slave-owner's actions as a matter of law. In other words, while retrospectively we can assign the proper responsibility in many cases, within the context of a political system where slavery is legally sanctioned, the determination of justice will be impossible, in fact. If a slave is *made* to do the various chores his master wants him to do, the resulting consequences, whether beneficial or harmful, are clearly not the slave's responsibility; the slave *might have* acted very differently had he been free to choose his own goals, though, of course, he *might have* done just what the slave-owner made him do The slave-owner himself cannot be held solely responsible for the results, for it is indeterminable whether he would have pursued his goal had slavery not been permitted by law. Whatever we might say about degrees of responsibility, what is clear is that, within a slavery sanctioning political system, the linking up of causes and effects regarding human action is rendered virtually impossible — impossible, that is, correctly. To be sure, a slave will most often be blamed when what he was told to do involved harmful consequences. If a slave is told to drive to town and in doing this he runs over a person, the slave will surely be held responsible; yet no one can say whether he would have undertaken the drive had he had the freedom to choose his course of action.

Furthermore, within the slave's private life the linking of causes with effects cannot be achieved. For we cannot tell just what personal tragedies were brought about by the slave owner's whim, as distinguished from consequences which followed decisions of the slave that he would have made whether living as freeman or slave. Illnesses, eccentric traits, over- or undernourishment and the variety of possible states men find themselves in may all be the results of this person's status as a slave; yet they may have nothing to do with it.

With serfdom the situation is not fundamentally different. Here again the society's legal system sanctions the conditions which serfs suffer and the responsibility for events and situations in which serfs are involved cannot be assigned justly within the system.

What is common to these is that the persons involved are not free to choose their own goals, the means of attaining them, etc., but are consistently interfered with by others. Furthermore, this condition is sanctioned by law and is officially considered the most appropriate. When persons are allowed by law — or caused by law — to suffer the consequences of actions actually performed by others, when citizens must forever live as cripples because the state used them in scientific experiments against their will, or when persons are legally punished for performing badly on a job which they were forced to take — then what we have is clearly a condition of injustice within the respective political systems. And what is characteristic about injustice *in law* is that it obtains from the *legal* sanction of the coercion of some people by others, that is, the *legal* unavailability of freedom. If anything is properly designated unjust, it is a situation where someone is either enjoying or suffering consequences not *caused* by him. (This, incidentally, may be applied to the enjoyment of gifts and inheritance; however, to prevent the resulting injustice would involve a more serious form of injustice, in most cases — the usurpation of the rights of individuals to distribute what is theirs to willing takers.)

To suffer unjustly is to suffer for something caused by another. To benefit unjustly is to benefit from something achieved by another at the other's expense. (Clearly, I may benefit from another's achievements, say his tasteful dressing habits or his use of the right kind of deodorant — nowhere do I delimit his own opportunity to enjoy the consequences of his acts, however.) With some risk we may put it thus: injustice denies, justice links cause and effect.

If a political or legal system fosters the denial of cause and effect, then it is, to that extent, unjust. In order to see whether our political system can be so characterized, and why, I will consider some of the results of the laws our political system incorporates. Clearly, the impact of these laws, if there is any, may not be so severe as to cause the degree of injustice — or the scope of it within the society — that we are familiar with in connection with the kind of societies depicted above where slavery and serfdom were legally sanctioned and supported practices of the society as a whole. Surely, in contemporary oppressive societies the discussion of justice, in a manner as directly critical as this chapter may turn out to be, would not be permitted. Yet, the simple fact that injustice has not (in America) reached a degree of pervasiveness we know it can reach and has reached elsewhere needn't soften our aversion to it, nor need it prompt us to dismiss the issue as insignificant in comparison to other harmful or evil situations which are also present.

Some of the laws which I will proceed to show to contribute to injustice are not all pervasive. There are ways in which one can avoid being submitted to the legal measures of a society. Yet, in the end, it is very hard to tell whether any member of society can escape the results of unjust laws, especially if some of these results may be welcome.

The broadest of the laws which are in this category — productive of injustice, that is — is the federal taxation law; it is broad because it covers all citizens who are engaged in any kind of productive enterprise. Yet, tax laws, while the broadest, are not the most consequential in impact. The law of our political system which fits the characterization of "most unjust" is the military conscription law, better known to all as the draft. Related but less widely known noted laws which can be seen as unjust are: laws and bills permitting the subsidization of businesses; laws imposing tariff restrictions and quotas against foreign businesses (indirect subsidization); the law prohibiting the ownership of gold; laws and bills which permit the dispensation of tax-payers' funds for selected scientific endeavors, cultural ventures, educational projects, etc.; zoning laws (which operate in many of the smallest communities of the country); *eminent domain* laws; property and sales tax laws; price fixing laws; anti-trust laws; "right-to-work" laws (which forbid business firms and labor groups to enter into free contractual agreements); censorship laws; conservation laws; laws against gambling, prostitution, or the use of drugs or narcotics; "public accommodation", "fair employment", "fair housing", and related laws aimed at integration; and thousands of others ... one could go on forever.

What is evident in the above list is that all of the laws included deviate from the purpose of government most widely accepted, namely the protection of the rights of individuals against the usurpation or abridgment of these rights by other men; in other words, the list includes laws which are "progressive" and render government an agent toward bringing about certain preferred human aims as against others, even when some members of the citizenry would prefer to neglect these aims. Laws, on the other hand, which protect the right of persons to act in line with their judgment, provided others' right to this is unimpinged, are not in the above list. The distinction, though a controversial one among philosophers interested in the concept of "human rights", is evident between progressive and protective laws. In this discussion, however, I cannot defend the distinction in detail. What I want to say about it is simply that the laws which I call protective are equally related to all citizens since they deal with the rights all human beings possess, with something which is common among the members of a society; the laws, however, which are in the list deal with the particular aims, goals, interests, difficulties, preferences and tastes of segments of the citizenry. For this reason I call them "progressive" laws: they contribute to the progress of these aims and goals; they do so, however, at the expense of other people's ability to make progress in the aims they have chosen or might have chosen for themselves.

The laws I have included in my list can be seen to comprise a substantial portion of what is called welfare legislation in our country (or elsewhere). It is the thesis of my paper that elements of the welfare state render the realization and attainment of justice in our society impossible. It is of no importance how the laws come into being—in principle they are no different from laws established by dictators, monarchs, the communist or fascist ruling groups, or a tribal lord, as regards their content; they serve to deprive individuals of their freedom to run their lives in line with their own judgments and capacities. It is unimportant here whether the people who are thus affected like or dislike their condition—the story of the happy southern slave is widely known and repeated by those who argue for the security and other "advantages" of slavery as against the benefits of justice. It is another issue entirely whether justice is to be preferred to other factors which could be secured in a political society.

Some have said that a just law has to satisfy no other requirement than that it is applicable to all citizens equally. This may indeed be an important rule (measure) for justice in the *application* of laws but it is not central to the productivity of justice by laws. A law, universally applied, which would hold guilty of murder not the person who did the killing but one who was in closest spatial proximity to him would be open to "just" application but be productive of injustice, nevertheless.

At this point let me return to the central purpose of my paper and give some illustration of the way in which some of the laws I listed are productive of injustice. Let us take taxation and see in what manner it produces injustice, i.e., in what way taxation renders the assignment of responsibility for various events, situations, circumstances, be they harmful or helpful to taxpayers, impossible. In what way, that is, do tax laws break the link between cause and effect in human action as this relates to the operation of the *assignment* of responsibilities?

When a person is taxed, he must, under threat of legal punishment (fines, jail, etc.), give up a certain amount of his earned income for purposes planned by past or present lawmakers. Here it is not important and relevant that *some* of these purposes may be shared by the taxpayer himself; he *must* support them—he does not enjoy the option of supporting them or not supporting them. What is central is that the taxpayer is *not free to withhold his support* from the purposes in point. In being deprived of his freedom to use his earned income for purposes designated wholly by him, the taxpayer's resources for advancing his own goals and purposes have been limited considerably.

The above is often rejected as a correct characterization of the nature of taxation on the following grounds: the citizen has gained immensely from many of the goals which have been achieved without his consent, in the past; for this reason it is only right and just that he should share the cost of these accomplishments. This is highly spurious. It is clearly unjust that a person, having been "given" something, for which he never had even the opportunity to ask, is made to share the cost of the "gift" at a later date, when he does not enjoy the option of rejecting the gift. The injustice arises out of the imposition of a responsibility upon the person when he does not share in the assumption of that responsibility. The reply that "He can leave the country any time he does not prefer the conditions" is equally spurious: after all it is merely an admission of injustice to tell a person that if he does not like the injustice he has still the option to escape the premises where it is the existing political or legal condition. Furthermore, if injustice is accepted within the legal system in principle, there is no ground for limiting it to those who wish to remain within the territory covered by that legal system; the next step may include the injustice of disallowing people to depart. (Such a measure is being contemplated in Great Britain as a result of the "brain drain" on the very grounds that the people who are leaving received their "free" education in England; it was, of course, the status quo within former "communist" countries.)

Considering that the issue at hand is the determination of whether justice is possible *within* a political system correctly characterized as a welfare state, we can proceed to investigate the manner in which taxation relates to this question. It should, however, be kept in mind that when one speaks of a society and its political system, it is a mistake to compare the situation to that of a social club or a fraternal organization. These latter are voluntarily formed groups which exist *within* a society and do, in fact, qualify very frequently as a "legal person" in their treatment by the law. The groups do *not* resemble society in many ways; most importantly, however, one is free to join or not to join them, free to take one's leave from them once his self-assumed debts to the organization have been paid, and the organization has no police force of itself but operates within the legal system of the society of which it is a part. Society, in general, does not have this character: its members are born such, in the main; one does not have the choice to assume one's "obligations" to the general society; society's governing body is not legally responsible to yet some greater or higher organization (with *its* own legal system). The fact that there are in existence different nation states and that there is some toying with the idea of a super-world- legal-system (world law, United Nations, etc.) does not invalidate my point; the governmental system preferred by someone is usually the same that he would like for the whole world to adopt. This is true of those who find the welfare state as the best kind of organization for human beings. This clearly is not the case with social and fraternal organizations such as the Lions or Kiwanis Clubs, the Red Cross, Optimists, and the thousands of other groups, each of which has its own special (group *of*) goals, aims, purposes, methods, interests, emphases, and so forth, representing the goals, etc., of its members, all of whom joined the groups presumably knowing of these and free to stay out. The contract theory of society, promulgated by political philosophers such as Jean-Jacques Rousseau, is a totally invalid conception of the state, both historically and theoretically.

Now, to return to the investigation, let me note that the taxpayer's own choices are not the determinants of what he will do. He will be forced to support programs — with his presumably honestly earned taxed income — he *might* never support were he free to refrain, and again, he *might* never undertake goals that he *would* have chose to pursue had he been free to do so. What he will do, in areas where he is free to act, will be the complicated outcome of choices with possibly crucial alternatives removed. With these alternatives lacking, it is now — when we attempt to attain justice in appraising him, both legally and otherwise — simply impossible to determine whether this lack did in fact contribute to the various events, circumstances, and states of affairs of his life.

Let us just imagine that the individual in question would have been free to invest his earnings in some business venture; he might have spent it on further education for himself or his children; he might have gambled it away — the possibilities are innumerable. *However* he *might* have spent his income had he been free to do so is indeterminable. What is more important is that equally indeterminable is *who* precisely is responsible for this condition in which we find the taxpayer.

If the abstract account given above has no impact, perhaps a more concrete one will. We can easily imagine a citizen who needs a new car because the motor of his old one is defective. He cannot, however, both pay his taxes and purchase a new vehicle. One morning he gets into an "accident" and suffers serious injuries, all as a consequence of the failure of his automobile. It is obvious that we cannot determine who is to be held responsible for the "accident" and the resulting injuries, etc. The individual could not buy a better car after he paid his taxes; furthermore, we cannot tell whether he *would* have bought one, had he been free to do so. So, the case is closed — with his earnings taken as taxes he certainly could not buy a car, and of his own free choice, with all his earnings, he could have, but might not have, bought one. The responsibility for the ensuing situation: indeterminable; a just appraisal of the situation: impossible.

It may be replied that "After all, the sheer fact that our social, economic and other interactions are complicated — not to mention the issue of psychological and sociological theories which make the matter even more complex — can contribute to numerous situations wherein the assignment of responsibility and, therefore, just appraisal, are rendered impossible." Granted the objection, there is a fundamental distinction between injustice which is the result of default, complications, and the like, and injustice which is brought about through the consciously planned actions of members of society, human beings, who might have refrained from making the laws which now contribute to the widespread injustice. From complications injustices arise which, however, are not planned to occur and are not desired, at any rate. From laws, which are not the result of the complexities of life itself but the ideas men have about dealing with some of these complexities, injustice can only be seen as avoidable.

The impact of taxation on a man's life is immense — yet, very few respected and prominent philosophers would argue that taxation is a contributing factor to injustice, taxation as an institution; they may argue that certain features of it produce injustice, of course. And this is not surprising. The interventions into the life of individuals in our society are so widespread and common, so well embedded, that they are virtually impossible to sort out. We may benefit from modeling the situation on what happens to the balls in a pinball machine: by the time they reach the end of their run they will have gone through various interferences, obstacles, shoves and pushes, all of which contribute to the end result. With a person the situation is a thousand times more complex due, in part, to the fact of human agency itself. The interferences are both caused and suffered by people, yet the intermediary, the law, serves to break the link between the interferer and the interfered unlike the pinball case and unlike, even, the case where a person suffers the interference not from the law but from a private individual or group, as in the case of theft, murder, extortion, and fraud. In these latter, interference has occurred but the law instead of perpetrating it, works to prevent injustice by linking the parties with their responsibility as best as can be done by human beings.

I have, thus far, been talking about just one of the hundreds of thousands of laws which can be characterized as depriving people of their freedom to pursue their own chosen ends, that is, laws which are productive of injustice. I will mention only one other law of this kind. This is conscription. The draft deprives a man of at least two years of his life if he is subject to it. Yet, there is absolutely no cogent justification for this law within a society the legal system of which has long rejected slavery as one of its features.

Conscription is defended most frequently on two grounds: (1) A person owes his country certain services in return for the benefits he has accrued by being born in the given country; (2) a country has a right to defend itself against possible aggression and such defense is unattainable without conscription. Both of these arguments uphold the welfare of the society (the state) as prior to the welfare of the individual citizens involved in providing that welfare. This is why I consider them classic arguments in behalf of the welfare state.

I have already dealt with argument (1) in connection with the alleged duty of a citizen to pay for services from which he gained benefits but which he never asked for. We saw that we were dealing with a variant of the social contract theory of society the model for which was provided by fraternal clubs and other private organizations which are indeed formed by contract.

Argument (2) is somewhat complicated because it presupposes a theory of nationhood still in question. Does any *kind* of country have the right to defend itself? What kind of right would it be that would grant legitimacy to a dictator's attempts, for instance, to defend the country which he rules? Presumably it would not be a moral right but a right of fiat, i.e., a right claimed by reason of rulership. If we are to talk of the right of a country or society to defend itself against aggressors, we must be open to the possibility that some countries cannot claim that right. This leads to problems of legitimate authority.

When does a government have legitimate authority to govern? Presumably when it is representative, when the governed have freely chosen to delegate to the government certain responsibilities to be carried out by that government. The crucial feature then is the freedom of the governed, the citizens. If conscription involves the usurpation of the rights of individuals to act in accordance with their own wishes, judgments, goals, etc. — the usurpation of freedom — then a government could not possibly conscript its citizens without losing its legitimacy in the process.

If, then, a country has the right to defend itself, it cannot do so by conscription without losing that right (by losing its legitimacy and, thereby, its right of exercising authority).

It is clear that conscription limits freedom of action: thus, the consequences of military conscription — or any other kind — are such that it is impossible to speak of the draftee as one who is responsible for his actions — his life is largely not in his own hands, the actions which he undertakes are not strictly his own, and the responsibility which ordinarily goes with the performance of actions by persons cannot, therefore, be his own either. Of course, some decisions and acts, once the limits of decision-making have been set by law, are the draftee's own. It would, therefore, be false to hold that he was responsible for *nothing*. Even this fact becomes obscured by the constant factor of interference, however.

It is obvious from the above that conscription is productive of grave injustices in society and renders the determination of responsibility — the linking of cause and effect in human action — impossible. In various more or less complicated and direct ways laws such as price-fixing, minimum-wage regulations, racial quotas, censorship, anti-gambling ordinances, and others are productive of similar injustices. Minimum-wage laws, for instance, force an employer to pay more for work than the market can bear; this can result in cutting down the workload; as a result people will be dismissed; others gain higher wages not as a result of better work but because of direction from the government; the higher wages can lead to higher prices, thereby eliminating the general effect of higher wages altogether. When companies collapse, employees are dismissed, children go hungry, illnesses cannot be cured for lack of funds, etc., etc. — thousands of consequences follow as a result of the initial governmental action which deprived men of their right to act in line with their own judgment; once again the link between the cause of the results and the results is broken and responsibility cannot be assigned.

Governmental subsidies to businesses are productive of similar results. And so are tariffs and quota systems, both of which deprive buyers in this country of alternative courses of action by force. When a manufacturer simply withholds his products from the market the situation is different, since it is he who makes the product and he, therefore, is not depriving anyone of something to which there exists a right. If Frank Sinatra refuses to sing to me when I offer to pay him for it, he is not depriving me of something to which I have a right. If another person stops him from singing by cutting his throat, both Sinatra and I have been interfered with. The government's tariff and quota policies can be modeled on the above example without any change in the essentials.

I believe that I have listed enough examples. Clearly, every law mentioned earlier and thousands of others can be put to similar scrutiny. What would be discovered is that at some point laws of this type interfere with the freedom of individuals in such a way that their activities will be impervious to being appraised concerning matters of responsibility, blame, desert, or accomplishment. And such a state of affairs renders justice within society an impossibility.

I have not ventured in this paper to suggest a governmental system within which the attainment of justice would be possible. That would certainly require not only another paper but several books. The fact that the society which I think would come closest to one within which justice is possible has been approximated within this country, with drastic contradictions evident within that approximation, would render the task of arguing for that sort of a system even more difficult than would ordinarily be the case. I am speaking, of course, about the system of government known as constitutional democracy, with government being limited to the duties of administering laws, protecting the innocent, and prosecuting the guilty. Within the society itself the police and the courts would represent the government, and for purposes of contact with other nations the military — pertaining to aggressors — and the diplomatic corps — relating to international legal matters — would represent the body and functions of such a government. The economy, morality, culture, sports, entertainment, education, etc., of the people would be their own individual business (or collective, whenever the collective body can be organized voluntarily). The financing of the government would be through the charging of fees for contracts which might be in need of legal backing and protection. Unlike a utopia, that kind of a system would secure justice for people, while it would be the people who would have to secure all else for themselves.

To argue for such a system would take us into ethics, metaphysics and, finally, epistemology. So I must refrain from doing this now. My present aim has been to discern whether justice is possible within the framework of a governmental system commonly known as the welfare state. The conclusion of my inquiry was that it is impossible to have both justice within a society and the governmental system of the welfare state.

As I mentioned, this conclusion does not establish the undesirability or impropriety of the welfare state. There might be other considerations which must be brought to bear upon those questions, considerations which might lead us to abandon justice as a desirable state of affairs within a legal system in favor of some other commodity, say security or happiness or racial purity.

Needless to say, *I* cannot think of any attribute of a community which is more important than justice. Thus I will confess my preference for a social system within which it is attainable. But a preference is not enough in philosophy; arguments are needed. To argue in favor of justice, as against other possible and competing benefits a governmental or legal system may provide, is necessary. Hopefully, despite the anti-political philosophy trend of contemporary philosophy, discussions related to such matters will attend to that question also.

Chapter VIII

Disputing Positive Rights

An influential idea in contemporary political philosophy is *positive rights*. It has been advanced by political thinkers on both the Right and the Left. In contrast to the theory of basic natural rights that John Locke developed, in terms of which every individual must be left free from the uninvited interventions of other persons, positive rights require us to provide resources and services to others who are in serious need.[1] Champions of natural rights consider positive rights as imposing involuntary servitude on us, by requiring that people be forced to provide services and benefits for others. Positive rights theorists claim, however, that these resources or services are due others, they are owed them. Positive rights arguably gave rise to the doctrine of entitlements among those involved in forging public policy.

Positive rights also check the principles of a fully free economy as understood in the classical liberal tradition of political economy. If people have such rights, one has no basis for refusing resources or services to them if they seriously need them. That implies that what people have in their possession may very well belong to others, including some of "their" skills, marketable attributes (e.g., good looks or talents). They could then be required by law — or, as the negative rights champions would have it, be conscripted or coerced — to serve the needs and wants of various other people regardless of their

[1] Lockean negative rights are to be established or shown to exist by reference to human nature. Whether such reference brings to light certain consequences that are to be achieved through respect for and protection of such rights or certain imperatives or duties regardless of consequences is of no significance in this discussion. Rights talk may be either consequentialist or non-consequentialist and the dispute about whether rights are negative or positive need not assume a position on that issue.

own choices. It is the government in a society that would secure the fulfillment of the obligations that arise from the existence of positive rights (that is, entitlements), either by means of direct performance (as when health care professionals would be mandated to provide their services to those who need them) or indirectly (as when government taxes the citizenry, usually along progressive lines, so as to provide resources or services for those who have a positive right or are entitled to them).

Furthermore, the doctrine of positive rights helps establish the case for government regulations, including of businesses. While negative rights proponents may construe such regulations as a type of prior restraint, supporters of positive rights tend to argue that others have a right to be provided with safety and risk prevention, and that it needs to be paid for by those who have the resources to do so. The customary idea of free trade is, thus, rejected, at least to the extent that some significant portion of what is ordinarily taken to be one's wealth is not one's own to allocate as one sees fit. (This matter surfaces during efforts to cut taxes — are the taxes the property of taxpayers or that of governments and simply held by taxpayers or citizens?)

Some argue that all rights are in fact positive rights.[2] This is because the means of protecting all rights would have to be the provision of government services that would secure or protect them, services that amount to a performance of certain sorts of actions (e.g., the police answering calls, judges ruling on conflicting claims, the military defending the country against attacks).

Some others, such as James P. Sterba, have maintained that positive rights exist because the possession of negative rights, by the very poor or unfortunate, entails or implies them. Sterba argues that "a libertarian ideal of liberty leads to a right to welfare."[3] That is because negative rights themselves are supported by the claim that without such rights no effort to live well is possible, if some cannot live well any-

---

[2]   Among them are Dworkin (1978), Shue (1970), Holmes & Sunstein (1999).

[3]   Sterba (1997), p. 102. It might be worth pointing out that there is nothing at all that is "Right" about libertarianism. The Right is conservative, even reactionary, and has traditionally rejected many of the tenets of classical liberalism or libertarianism, even its principled adherence to the right to private property and free trade. One need but think of Pat Buchanan's vociferous opposition to free trade to confirm this point or, if one wants more respectable evidence, of Edmund Burke's and other conservatives' (e.g., Russell Kirk's) criticism of individualism, a central feature of the libertarianism at issue here. Indeed, by some accounts libertarianism is Left because it is close to Enlightenment ideas that champion reason and science.

way, and only if others provide them with resources will they manage to make the effort to live well, then surely they do have a right to those resources, a right that is positive now, not negative.[4]

There are certain insurmountable problems with all these views. Shue, Holmes and Sunstein, who believe that we have positive rights to the services of the state and, thus, to the earnings of taxpayers who must pay for these services, fail to show that any right to being provided with protection exists without a prior negative right to liberty which one exercises so as to elect to have it protected and then delegates to an agency, such as government or a body guard, to do the protection for oneself. They ignore the "consent of the governed" provision in the establishment of government and so they treat that institutions as unproblematic or explainable by reference to positive rights. Yet, as negative rights theorists maintain, it is through the exercise of negative rights — say, the right to enter into a contract or form a compact — that some derivative positive rights are created.[5]

Yet, to obtain protection for something presupposes that one has the right to liberty to take such actions that will produce it. This right

---

[4]   There are many approaches taken to defending the libertarian stance. Some that are advanced mainly by economists do not involve rights, only the overall efficiency of free institutions. Others take rights as a starting point, while yet others rest negative rights on prior ethical theory about the responsibility to strive for excellence. Sterba has argued against those libertarians who take either liberty or the right to liberty as crucial in their positions. Others have argued against negative rights that they rest on shaky foundations and thus cannot be justified. For example, Adrian Bardon (2000) rejects what he takes to be the two important arguments for property rights, based on autonomy (or respect) and on desert, respectively, he finds in Robert Nozick. The natural rights position relies on neither of these but on the unique identity and sovereignty of human beings that makes them unavoidable for involuntary servitude or public use and on their nature as free and morally responsible, thus in need of the *moral space* Nozick mentions so as to make decisions about right and wrong conduct. If there is any ground for respect, it lies in the fact that one's humanity imposes on everyone the task of making life supporting decisions. If there is any desert, it comes from the routine but not necessary requirement that assets and resources one owns need to be allocated effectively, productively. Yet, initial assets — talent, beauty, inherited wealth — need not be deserved, only be a part of one's identity as the individual person one is. It is one's right to one's life that justifies others' obligation not to intrude on one, not that one has earned special moral respect or deserved the property one happens to have. This should be evident from the fact that it is absurd to think that one deserves one's life, as if one had struggled to be born is now rewarded with freedom for having done so.

[5]   For how children's positive rights emerge, see Machan (1992).

amounts to voluntarily combining with others for the purpose of gaining self-protection by establishing a government or similar authority that may act to protect rights because that authority has be freely delegated to it by rights possessors. That original right, however, is a negative one, requiring that others abstain from intervening in one's affairs.

So, the services of government, according to negative rights theorists, are something people must freely choose to obtain, by their consent to be governed, and they do not have a natural right to those services prior to having freely established such a rights protecting institution.

Sterba, in turn, makes the mistake of generalizing into a principle of law what amounts to a rare moral emergency case – namely, when some innocent people are totally helpless and should obtain resources by stealing them. *Pace* Sterba, those extraordinary circumstances do not generate any rights for people, although those who attempt to meet them by way of stealing might very well be forgiven because of their very limited options.

The doctrine of positive rights has an appeal to those who are faced with the theory of government that guides American law and politics. This theory is a source of promise to their efforts to elevate what people badly need to what they have rights to. America was founded on a theory that every individual human being has the unalienable right to, among other things, life, liberty and property. These rights that John Locke first identified – following several centuries of political and legal thinking during which various theorists have begun to identify them more or less precisely – are, as noted already, negative. Those political theorists who consider it important to retain some elements of the political outlook which Locke's position displaced, namely, the view that people belonged to the country – were, in fact, *subjects* of the country's head, the king, not sovereign citizens – found a way to use the concept of human – but now positive, not negative – rights to advance their position.[6] They appropriated some elements of the concept of negative human individual rights and attached it to the idea of needs or important values that people often have so as to manage to secure what others might provide for them. That element is that if one has rights, one is not just

[6]   For the most thorough theorist now arguing for the idea that *we belong to* – and are not only *members of* – our communities, see Charles Taylor, (1985), pp. 187–210. This belonging is akin to the way the heart, liver or nose is a part of the body and isn't a member of it; so, by this account, human individuals are a part of society, not free members who may elect to cancel their membership.

authorized to but in fact ought to secure their protection. As the U. S. Declaration of Independence so succinctly put it, it is "to secure these rights [that] governments are instituted among men, deriving their just powers from the consent of the governed." Now if we also have positive rights, then governments would also have the task to secure them, namely, the performance by us of those actions that will provide what others have a positive right to.

Probably the most serious problem of positive rights arises from how they compare with how negative rights are understood in the Lockean natural rights classical liberal tradition. In that framework a conflict of (justified, true) rights claims cannot exist. In this political framework when a claim is made as to someone's having a basic (not, however, legal) right, this claim may be checked for whether it is true by reference to a correct understanding of human nature. That such an understanding is possible is itself a controversial issue that need not concern us for now.[7]

Why is the Lockean approach to rights superior to the positive rights approach? Because the natural rights position understands human nature to rest on our correct grasp of an aspect of reality. With the understanding of human nature and the character of human social life we discover that morality and politics have emerged as uniquely human concerns in reality. For example, we learn by the use of our reason, as Locke puts it, that men and women ought to strive to succeed in their lives but face avoidable threats from others who refuse to accept mutually supportive conditions for striving. In this light we need to answer a question concerning ourselves, namely, "How we ought to live?" This is because human beings lack the instinctual, innate or hard-wired information that will just take care of their living for them, that will secure their successful living automatically. Furthermore, given our social nature, which Lockeans and other classical liberals and libertarians by no means reject[8] — *pace* the claims of Taylor and other communitarians who claim that this tradition assumes an atomistic idea of human

---

[7] The skepticism here, as in many other cases, stems mainly from a wholly unrealistic conception of what it takes to know something. With the idea that when we know something we have the clearest, most self-consistent, and most complete conceptualization possible to date of what it is we supposedly know — in contrast to the idea that when we know something we have a final, perfect, understanding of it — the most serious and destructive kind of skepticism does not arise. I discuss this in Machan (1982).

[8] I discuss the mistake Taylor and other communitarians make in such an ascription of atomism to the classical liberal, libertarian school in Machan (1998a, 1998c).

nature[9] — we need to answer the question "How should we organize ourselves in communities?"

As per the Lockean negative rights framework, in both these human normative spheres, ethics and politics, we are still, as in the sciences, dealing with reality, albeit a special dimension of it. So here, just as anywhere else — say in economics and biology — no conflict is tolerable between true claims.[10]

Furthermore, the natural rights classical liberal tradition identifies the rights, for example, to life, liberty and property as basic *for human community organization* but not, however, for human life at the personal, non-political level.[11] No concern with rights can arise on a desert island for Robinson Crusoe. Only among strangers, in larger communities, does the issue of how we ought to treat one another become pre-eminent and thus of great significance for political and legal purposes.

None of this holds for positive rights. The very fact of scarcity introduces inherent conflicts between allegedly true positive rights claims. And, of course, for those who accept both negative and positive rights as basic to human community life, the conflicts multiply. For example, the negative right of a doctor to liberty is inherently in conflict with the positive right of a patient to health care. So, a serious problem of positive rights theories is that positive rights are unable to function as fundamental criteria of political justice, criteria that serve to assess the merits of claims citizens make concerning their

[9]   Taylor (1993), Bellah et al. (1985), and Spragens (1982). For a critical examination of the misattribution of atomism to classical liberal and libertarian politics, see Skoble (1992).

[10] True ethical and political — including basic rights — claims are no less factual and thus no less in need of conforming to the criteria of consistency and coherence as those in the natural sciences. The reason is ultimately metaphysical, in the last analysis, justified in Aristotle's defense of the Law of Non-Contradiction, a defense that still stands and the challenge of which is unavoidably self-defeating. For the details of this line of defense of the Lockean rights stance, see Machan (1989).

[11] This conflicts with Taylor's claim to the contrary. Taylor says the following about the Lockean position, something quite wrong in light of Locke's own reference to a law of nature — namely, ethics that our reasoning faculty can grasp "if we but consult it" — that is prior to and required for the conceptualization of negative rights:

   Theories which assert the primacy of rights are those which take as the fundamental, or at least a fundamental, principle of their political theory the ascription of certain rights to individuals which deny the same status to a principle of belonging or obligation, that is a principle which states our obligation as men to belong to or sustain society, or a society of a certain type, or to obey authority or an authority of a certain type. (p. 188)

range of authority in society. Instead, with positive rights, since they are in mutual conflict and since they also conflict with other rights many positive rights theorists accept as having at least some standing, there cannot be the rule of law, only the rule of rulers who will decide which of the inherently conflict rights will be protected. This way the whole point of rights as fundamental to a political society is lost and we are back to the arbitrary rule of government, be it monarchic, democratic or whatever.

Any *bona fide* political system must be organized in large measure so as to protect the rights to life, liberty and, in the practical respect of both of these, the right to private property (see Machan [2002]). Thus any political rights – to be free to engage in decision making *vis-a-vis* political matters – must not violate those basic rights. Political rights include the right to vote, serve in government, take part in the organization of political campaigns, etc. Practically speaking, the exercise of one's political rights may have an impact on who governs, various internal rules of government, and the organization of political processes. But there is no political right within the negative rights framework to override anyone's right to life, liberty or property. Any evidence of some community's legal system overriding these rights is *ipso facto* evidence of the corruption of that system from a *bona fide* civil polity into one of arbitrary (even if majority) rule. Indeed, one of the failings of contemporary conservative legal theory is not to appreciate the intimate connection between Lockean individualism and democracy. Because of this, many think democracy may trump our basic rights.

The main reason that the American founders established a government that was to secure our rights is that they agreed with Locke and a few others throughout human history that justice requires that communities fit human beings as moral agents, with their personal responsibility to govern their own lives. And they also thought that the only chance of government by law, and thus justice, is the institution of a constitution that contains the criteria for justice, namely, basic rights that are coherent and consistent, that apply to all and can be protected for all.

With the introduction of the conceptual contrivance known as positive rights, it turns out to be in principle impossible for government to govern by a set of consistent standards, standards that had been provided with reasonable completeness by the theory of individual rights. Positive rights must be in inherent conflict. And they conflict, most of all, with our basic negative rights to life, liberty and property.

In the last analysis, the doctrine of positive rights leaves government free to impose its arbitrary standards of government — one day it is to help AIDS research, the next to foster the arts by supporting Public Broadcasting Service, yet another day the provision of our national interest[12] in oil in the Middle East and then the next day it is to solve the problem of immoderate smoking habits among the citizenry. No standards of restraint apply — indeed, as in a fascistic system, anything goes the leaders think is important. The only difference is that the leaders still abide some modicum of democracy.

As we judge communities across the globe, we must keep in mind that what is comparatively best is not always the best that is in fact possible. Thus we can affirm the greater merits of certain political communities or countries despite their evident violation of basic rights. Just as in personal assault cases we can distinguish between major and minor cases, as well as those in between, we can also tell when communities rest on principles that render those systems entirely corrupt, those that simply are confused and messy, and those that come reasonably near to meeting the standards of basic human rights. In a formal way we already apply this method of judging communities, even if not for all purposes. We should go much farther and apply it more strictly and substantively, including as we appraise our own country's laws.

The doctrine of positive rights is seriously, probably fatally, flawed. With its abandonment a more promising idea may gain currency. This is that instead of positive rights, there are values some are in dire need of and some of those who can relieve them may have the moral responsibility to do so, one they ought freely to choose to carry out. Without the impossible dream of everyone having the right to such relief, as an enforceable obligation from others, this more promising albeit non-utopian view will gain greater impact, thereby fostering the solution of problems that the advocates of positive rights only pretend to tackle, however benign their intentions may be.

---

[12] In contrast to national *security*, which is but a generalization from the individual security from negative rights violations that citizens may elect to obtain via government.

CHAPTER IX

Can Commerce Inspire?

> Money, which represents the prose of life, and which is hardly spoken of in parlors without an apology, is, in its effects and laws, as beautiful as roses.
>
> Ralph Waldo Emerson

> Aristippus championed only the body, as though we had no soul, Zeno championed only the soul, as though we had no body. Both were flawed.
>
> Michael de Montaigne

It is no exaggeration that the fully free society as understood in this discussion has been closely linked with commerce. It has often been dubbed a commercial or bourgeois society and roundly condemned for it because it is believed, widely, both by those on the Right and those on the Left, that there is something impoverished about it, it lacks soul, it is too shallow and hedonistic.[1]

Commerce and Its Dubious Reputation

Given its reputation in many of the popular renditions of world religions and philosophies, commerce wouldn't be expected to inspire. Most of those who comment on such matters do not consider engaging in commerce to contain any measure of nobility or moral worth, but merely some practical or instrumental value.[2] For example, the actual transaction in a purchase is taken to be of instrumental importance; however, most people hold that commerce fails to lend our life any dimension of worth.

---

* Originally published in Nicholas Capaldi, ed., *Business & Religion: A Clash of Civilizations* (M&M Scrivener Press, 2005).

---

[1]   A very good case in point is Daniel Bell (1996).
[2]   For more on this, see Machan & Chesher (1999).

Many go a lot further and declare commerce outright vicious. Charles Baudelaire, for example, states that, "Commerce is satanic, because it is the basest and vilest form of egoism. The spirit of every businessman is completely depraved." And then he adds, very revealingly, that, "Commerce is *natural*, therefore *shameful*".[3] And Arthur Miller remarks, a century later and in America where commerce is relatively hospitably treated, that "His was a salesman's profession, if one may describe such dignified slavery as a profession ..." (Miller, 1995/1996).

Indeed, one problem with commerce in most cultures is that it is thought to be mundane to the core. There is unease about commerce throughout the religious community in light of what most take to be religion's main concern, namely, striving for everlasting salvation. This is often interpreted to mean, for example, that the rich cannot gain entrance to heaven, that money lenders are the worst lot abusing the temple, that it would not profit one to gain the world but lose one's soul, etc.

Such ideas are not necessarily the best way to understand the relationship between religion and commerce. In especially those faiths that regard the earthly life of human beings vital to care for — or to use an Aristotelian locution, ones that implore us to flourish here on earth — commerce could well occupy a very respectable, honorable role. After all, it is through commerce that we most effectively exercise the moral virtue of prudence vis-à-vis the requirements of our temporal lives. In this respect, as I point out in this discussion, commerce is no less significant for a good human life than medicine or engineering.

Yet, as will be seen, my position is different from the positions of those, such as George Gilder, who hold that commerce lends our lives a measure of worth because it involves a variety of (at least consequentialist) altruism by requiring the commercial agent to pay close attention to what benefits his or her trading partner or customer (Gilder, 1981). This idea, championed among religious defenders of commerce and capitalism, maintains that when we engage in commerce or the profession of business, we are benefiting other people, as well as ourselves, and it is the former that is morally ennobling, with the latter remaining morally suspect but sufficiently moderated so as not to amount to rank greed (see, e.g, Lapin [2004]).

---

[3] Baudelaire (1957, p. 51). The connection between one's basic philosophical view and what the person thinks of business is clear from the second observation — deeming what is *natural* to be, for that very reason, *shameful*.

Aristotelian-Thomist Ethics and Commerce

I argue, instead, that the mainstream position about commerce requires serious reconsideration in light of human nature and the morality of self-perfection or eudaimonia.[4] If it is true, as Aristotle, Thomas Aquinas, and some others have held, that a central normative element of our humanity — that is to say, a fundamental ethical responsibility we all have — is to achieve flourishing in our lives, and our lives substantially involve creative, productive connectedness to the natural world that surrounds us, and if commerce facilitates this connectedness, then commerce *qua* self-development and the pursuit of prosperity occupies a far more elevated role in our lives than is testified to by many prominent world views.

Of course, the value of commerce as a means for enriching our lives and enhancing culture can be appreciated even apart from showing that it contains moral worth in and of itself, as a form of human activity. One need but peruse the windows of most stores at a contemporary mall in a thriving commercial society to recognize that they contain creations and products that are awe-inspiring for their combined beauty and usefulness. One might even regard the contemporary mall as a surrogate museum of contemporary culture. It is possible to just wander around, as one does in a museum, and admire the thousands of different items offered up not just for consumption or use, but also for apprehension, appreciation, and admiration. Inasmuch as this is the routine result of commerce, one should join George Mason University Professor Tyler Cowan who argues that free trade is not only efficient and moral but often also quite beautiful, even as it is also destructive of old and outmoded attachments people have formed in their lives (Cowan, 2003).

Why Commerce Is Ethical

But let me now turn to the issue of whether commerce may be constitutive of an ethical, flourishing life, just as moral virtue is constitutive of happiness in Aristotle's and Thomas Aquinas' ethical thought. Within this ethical framework the moral virtues, when practiced conscientiously, help to guide us toward happiness in life, but they are themselves an aspect of the happiness they produce. Choosing to be prudent, honest, temperate, generous, and just amounts to choosing ways of living and the combined result of such choices is likely to be happiness.

[4] The most astute modern development of this Aristotelian ethical position is found in Norton (1976).

Choosing prudently to enhance our lives here on earth, including by means of thoughtful trade, provides us with a source of confidence, efficaciousness, which itself constitutes the flourishing that improves a human life so much.

Of course, there are many adjacent features of commerce that show its beneficial elements: it often is a first step toward friendship, at least a friendship of pleasure or even utility, but sometimes even a friendship of virtue (one often comes to know another person in the course of trading with him or her); romance, too, can commence from a trade relationship; learning, too, is often facilitated by trade, as is aesthetic enjoyment; on the international front, the absence of war between societies the citizens of which are actively trading with each other is a very serious, even inspiring benefit of trade. Such results, of course, can be found quite apart from trade. But that is true of many other ways in which good things come about in human intercourse — for example, athletics, science, education and politics.

But perhaps the most inspiring aspect of commerce is the realization upon reflection that it is such a widespread contributor to human well being here on earth. It is no accident that every newspaper reports on business in each of its issues, no less so than it does on entertainment, education, athletics and other positive aspects of human living. More directly, commerce inspires by contributing to one's, one's family's and associates' well being. Contrary to the view sometimes associated with Aristotle, namely, that retail trade has only instrumental value, there is actually an Aristotelian understanding of commerce that sees it as engendering human self-confidence, pride. When one embarks upon successful dealings, one is demonstrating competence in earning a living within a complicated social framework.

Money as "The Prose of Life"

Martha Nussbaum has argued that, "The Aristotelian holds that money is merely a tool of human functioning and has value in human life only insofar as it subserves these functionings. More is not always better, and in general, the right amount is what makes functioning best." (Nussbaum [1992], p. 231.) Actually, if this were true, then all human virtues could be demeaned as well, since their worth consists, at least in Aristotle, in their contribution to human happiness. Nussbaum's account clearly suggests that business professionals can only earn moral credit through deeds other than what their profession calls for. These would be *pro bono* contributions such as philanthropic and charitable deeds, funding of libraries, museums, athletic events or art centers, and not contributions as they function in the capacity of business professionals.

This is a mistake. Before I explain, let me turn, however, to the point Nussbaum attributes to Aristotle about money. Here it is Aristotle who was making a mistake, probably because of his general disdain for physical labor and whatever came close to it, such as earning money, as well as his view that only those crafts involving strict determinacy — that is to say, a beginning, middle and end — are worthwhile. In the case of money-making, there is no determinate conclusion to the task, thus it isn't possible to evaluate it as one can evaluate the work of a tailor, miller, architect or playwright.

Yet Aristotle fails to note that there are many tasks that resemble money-making, such as farming, exploration, scientific research, and philosophy, none of which involve determinate tasks, but instead, indeterminate, endless activities.

It is also worth noting that being a contributor to human well being, money (or the making of it) is not necessarily "*merely* a tool of human functioning." By Aristotle's own account of the relationship between means and ends — for example in how the moral virtues are means to human happiness — the earning of money can be constitutive of human functioning. To wit, someone who is skilled at making money is an effective contributor to his or her economic well being which, in turn, can contribute to his or her overall flourishing.

Money may be a means of exchange but it is more than that, as well. It is an easily and widely recognized representative of productivity. Money is also a fungible good, like a movie, theater, concert or any other kind of ticket with which one is able to obtain what one needs and wants. (Professor Walter Williams has called it "a certificate of performance" on a recent radio program.[5]) Obtaining such a ticket enables one to gain the value of seeing a movie, going to a play, concert or museum, all of them valuable experiences. If money makes this possible, then the activity that gains it cannot be without merit and can, indeed, be constitutive of a measure of success in human living.

Furthermore, an enormous benefit of money is its already mentioned fungibility. Most of us are good at doing this or that, can flourish at our professions, and yet because of earning money rather than engaging in barter, we are able to contribute to the advancement of innumerable other tasks we would not be capable of promoting

---

[5]   The Rush Limbaugh Program, Friday, November 19, 2004.

directly. So, we send money to support the local theater group or orchestra, help some research effort to find a cure for some disease, further our children's and sometimes others' education, promote some idea by giving to a think tank, etc. Money can be earned in tasks at which we are good and then contributed to advance numerous other purposes. (Of course, money can also be spent on frivolity and degradation, yet corruption of any activity is a risk for free moral agents.) Those, therefore, who can help us improve our money earning capacities — that is, our wealth — namely, professionals in business, certainly are justified in taking pride in what they are doing, no less so than are those who can help us improve our health, so that we can then devote ourselves to various other worthy tasks.

Prudence Grounds the Worth of Commerce

Accordingly, I am proposing here that commercial skill or savvy is best understood as an activity that is guided by prudence, which is an Aristotelian (not Hobbesian) moral virtue and is, thus, constitutive of human happiness.[6] Too many thinkers have discounted commerce as a source of inspiration, as a source of ennoblement, even — while electing to credit other endeavors such as art, science, education, and the rest with the capacity to inspire — of possessing the worthy attributes I claim commerce possesses as well. Professional practitioners are worthy persons in these other activities not only because of what they produce. An educator, for example, is honored because of the merits of what he or she does, of his or her calling or vocation, not only because of the valuable results that stem from it. Perhaps this is, in part, because professions such as education, medicine, law, farming and the like can all be cast as *services to others* and one can, thus, discount the fact that many pursue them for the rewards they bring to the agent — the educator, scientist, artist, attorney, and so forth. But it is no accident that when one considers a profession, one seeks some activity that is self-fulfilling, that realizes one's talents and the vision one has of one's future life, even apart from how others may benefit from it. Some may indeed seek work by asking where one's efforts may be most urgently needed by others but many ask, also, how their own life will be enhanced by this work. Many enter a profession because of early affinity for the kind of skill it requires or because some early experience has shown it to be important and personally appealing.

---

[6]   See Machan (forthcoming).

Commerce and the Spirited Life

Accordingly, just as any other worthy craft, skill and profession can inspire, that is to say, result in a spiritually enhanced life — via pride and self-esteem from the knowledge one is doing well at something worthwhile — so has commerce and its professional arm, business, the capacity to produce inspiration.[7] Of course, this may well be thwarted by widespread disdain for the craft or skill, just as the reputation of, say, the performing arts at one time tended to dampen such enhancement for the actors who were the targets of snobbery and derision.

To these considerations someone is very likely to respond along the following lines: "Well, yes, commerce helps one to get what one needs and desires and this is certainly important, but is it really a moral or ethical matter? After all, each of us wants the best for himself — this is only natural. What you've shown is that commerce helps us do this and we shouldn't put it down. OK, but why is it so admirable, indeed moral, to help oneself? After all, even if prudence is a virtue, it is but one of them, and most of the others, when exercised, seem more admirable: courage in saving others seems more admirable than courage in saving oneself, and generosity seems almost totally other-directed ..."

This is of course very much a mainstream approach to commerce, not at all in line with the Aristotelian-Thomist approach I have been urging in this discussion. Actually, prudence is rarely seen as a moral virtue in our neo-Kantian framework on matters of morality,[8] yet in Aristotle prudence is a central virtue — one reason it is often called the first of the *cardinal* virtues — and Thomas Aquinas continued to treat it as such. "They are called cardinal (Latin: *cardo*, hinge) virtues because they are hinges on which all moral virtues depend. These are also called moral (Latin: *mores*, fixed values) because they govern our actions, order our passions, and guide our conduct according to faith and reason."[9] Another understanding of prudence

---

[7]   Needless to say, all crafts, skills and professions can be corrupted by misuse and malpractice. Business is by no means unique in this. See Machan & Chesher (1999, 2003), for the professional ethical implications this approach to business yields.

[8]   Actually Kant liked commerce but as far as gaining moral credit for prudence, his austere conception of deontological morality, wherein anything one is inclined to do would not be morally meritorious, led to the moral evisceration of prudence.

[9]   http://www.secondexodus.com/html/catholicdefinitions/cardinalvirtu es.htm

is "right reason", and that indicates just how fundamental is the moral virtue we are discussing here — the very basis of moral or ethical thinking, given that in the Aristotelian-Thomist tradition such thinking concerns how one achieves excellence in one's life as a rational animal (Norton [1976]; see also Machan [1998a]).

It is because of the neo-Hobbesian materialist ontology that prudence became demoted to a mere inclination, which is how Kant and subsequent moral philosophy tended to treat it (Den Uyl [1991]).

Some may have reservation about my treatment of Kant who was, in fact, a proponent of commercial society. Kant and Hegel both see the commercial transformation of the world as the act of sprit in its expression of freedom. Arguably both Aristotelians and Kantians see the nobility of this life.

Christian asceticism, by the way, may be a virtue in a world of extreme scarcity, but it becomes a vice in a world where we *can* overcome poverty; perhaps some members of the religious community failed to note the context within which asceticism made sense; perhaps they are confusing wealth with "spiritual" poverty when we all know that "spiritual" poverty is a psychological condition and not an economic condition. In short, they are confusing a time-sensitive economic condition with religious dogma. They tell us that the pursuit of wealth is bad but then they want us to distribute more of it to the poor. For instance, one could become a saint in the Middle Ages by giving one's wealth to the poor, not, however, by destroying one's wealth. Creating wealth for oneself and others is the modern counterpart.[10]

Religion and Commerce Revisited

Where does this leave us with respect to the issue of the relationship between religion and commerce? As suggested before, it depends on the conception of the good human life that a given faith embraces. If, for example, a faith views the type of earthly life that is proper to us as ascetic and demeans the human body as an obstacle to focusing on what is important, then commerce will naturally occupy a lowly place in that faith. That this is how many understand the relationship is indisputable. Church leaders of many faiths preach the doctrine of unselfishness, self-denial, even self-abnegation from which they derive a view of commerce as representing no more than rank greed in human life.

---

[10]   I thank Nicholas Capaldi for pointing some of this out to me.

Adam Smith, the founder of modern economic science and a moral philosopher in his own right made the following poignant observations related to this issue:

> Ancient moral philosophy proposed to investigate wherein consisted the happiness and perfection of a man, considered not only as an individual, but as the member of a family, of a state, and of the great society of mankind. In that philosophy the duties of human life were treated of as subservient to the happiness and perfection of human life. But when moral, as well as natural philosophy, came to be taught only as subservient to theology, the duties of human life were treated of as chiefly subservient to the happiness of a life to come. In the ancient philosophy the perfection of virtue was represented as necessarily productive to the person who possessed it, of the most perfect happiness in this life. In the modern philosophy it was frequently represented as almost always inconsistent with any degree of happiness in this life, and heaven was to be earned by penance and mortification, not by the liberal, generous, and spirited conduct of a man. By far the most important of all the different branches of philosophy became in this manner by far the most corrupted. (Smith, 1936, p. 726.)

On the Wrong Path with Kant

As hinted above, the major philosopher with religious orientation who could well exemplify Smith's point is Kant, even though his work followed Smith's. In Kant the phenomenal — mundane, earthly — life seemed to lack moral significance because it followed the laws of classical physics. In this sphere there is no free will and so there is no genuine choice, which is a prerequisite of morality. (It is Kant, after all, who stressed the importance of the philosophical motto, "'ought' implies 'can'", meaning that only if one is free to choose, it is meaningful to ascribe moral responsibilities to that individual.)

Accordingly, the Kantian approach to ethics stresses the good will, a kind of ineffable spiritual faculty that is free because it is of the noumenal (nonmaterial) dimension of reality. The only reason some room for prudence exists in Kantian ethics is that it represents a needed concern, albeit virtually instinctive, with the well being of the agent.

In this framework commercial savvy is a matter of natural inclination or instinct, not of good will and judgment. The result is that commerce lacks moral significance.

As noted already, an Aristotelian-Thomist understanding of morality could well cast commerce in a very different light. In Christianity there is room for serious, conscientious attention to flourishing on earth. Jesus became man in part to make this evident to the faithful, or so some have interpreted the faith.

Secular But Not Materialist

Apart, however, from the murky disputes surrounding religious faiths, all hampered, I think, because of the epistemic problem of infirm grounds[11] — faith is more of a commitment to a belief as distinct from belief arising from consideration of evidence and reasoning — the commercial aspect of human social life certainly isn't negligible. Such a practical sphere — no less than medicine, engineering, farming, and other crafts and trades that ought to be done well — deserves respect and so do those who are its conscientious practitioners. With this made possible by rethinking the nature of commerce, self-respect and moral pride shouldn't be far behind.

One hazard, though, of taking such a secular approach to commerce is that it could collapse into sheer reductive materialism, as exhibited in the foundational philosophical work of Thomas Hobbes and the subsequent writings of scientific economists.[12] Indeed, one impetus for Kant's taking morality away from the phenomenal world is that he thought if this was where morality would have to be found, there would be no place for it at all. There is no freedom of choice in classical mechanics, only efficient causation, which leaves no room for making better or worse decisions, despite torturous efforts by some so called "compatibilist" philosophers to reconcile determinism with moral responsibility.[13]

Reconsidering Aristotelian Causation

Instead of accepting the reductive materialist ontology that leaves no room for morality in the realm of nature, a revitalized Aristotelian approach recommends itself. This approach understands that reality is all one system but not all one substance. There are emergent

---

[11] Gary Wills notes, in a related context, that "Natural reason must use natural tools to deal with this question — philosophy, neurobiology, psychology, medicine." See "The Bishops vs. the Bible", *The New York Times*, June 27, 2004, WK, p. 13.

[12] For more along these lines, see Machan (1990).

[13] See, for example, Dennett (1984). For why this approach is hopeless, see Machan (2000 and 1974).

qualities in reality, and human life has developed attributes and capacities that make ample room for significant choices, many of which become subject to moral assessment.

Moreover, this approach understands causality so that not all causes must be of the same type. It is only natural that under the reductive materialist position all causes must be efficient ones, since only one kind of entity exists, namely, matter-in-motion, and thus only one kind of productivity can be found in nature. But if there exists a plurality of beings, some very simple — call them sub-atomistic — and others very complex — call them human — then room may be found for what Aristotelian morality requires, namely, agent causation.

This is the kind of causation ordinarily accepted, one that makes sense of people achieving things: Mozart composing music, Rembrandt creating paintings, Frank Lloyd Wright designing buildings, and Wittgenstein producing puzzling philosophy. Of course, it also makes room for terrorists wreaking havoc, murderers destroying human lives, arsonists making destructive fires and so on.[14]

Among what such an ontological outlook (that is, one bearing on the *type of being* something is) embraces is, then, humanity's creative capacity. And part of that capacity is to engage in responsible commerce and business. Insofar as it is morally proper for human beings to secure for themselves a prosperous life, their creative capacities may be exercised in service of this objective. How the creative capacities are exercised will, of course, be subject to moral evaluation. Just as in medicine it is generally morally praiseworthy to pursue health, those who do this professionally should also do it ethically — ergo the field of medical ethics. The same is true of other professions that are morally unobjectionable.

So there is a twofold moral issue afoot here: first, the moral standing of the profession and, second, whether the conduct of those who practice it is ethical. This is the same with the profession of business. The main challenge in the theological treatment of this matter is epistemic — how can we know that the tenets of a faith affirming, for example, the significance of one's earthly life are true. The main challenge in the secular treatment is ontological — could there exist a being such that it can choose freely and be morally responsible.

---

[14] For more on the scientific thesis about the creative agency of human individuals, see Sperry (1983) and his more technical paper, Sperry (1976).

The Secular Spiritual Case Outlined

Since I have made the attempt to demonstrate that the secular treatment can yield a positive answer to the ontological question, I will merely summarize the results. Reality is not all the same but there are fundamentally different types of entities of which it is comprised. Depending on the type of being something is, it will contain different causal powers. In the case of human beings, those causal powers are best understood as creative, so that the human agent can be the cause of some of its own behavior, the cause of its actions. The most evident sphere of such causation is evidently mental — human beings can initiate the process of conceptual thinking. And this is what grounds the quality of their actions and institutions.

The case for this position isn't one that yields deductively certain conclusions but, instead, theses that best explain the phenomena we are aware of, including in association with all varieties of human life. Just as in the case of criminal trials, it is the theory that best explains the evidence at hand that should carry the day; therefore, in such areas of substantive philosophy what explains the phenomena most parsimoniously should carry conviction.[15]

In the absence of an epistemically compelling theological case for a moral perspective on human life and on the field of commerce and the profession of business, and with a secular one available that does reasonable justice to the undeniable moral dimension of human life (which reductive materialists views cannot do), it seems to me that the case pertaining to the spirit — character, values, and highest aspirations — of the individuals embarking upon commerce makes the best sense. It is true, it seems to me, without a reasonable doubt.

Given, then, this conception of spirituality or, rather, *spiritedness*, there is little doubt that commerce and its professional arm, business, can be viewed as every bit as much imbued with spirituality as are medicine, education, science, art and politics.

---

[15] For more, see Machan (1974, 2000).

Bibliography

Bardon, Adrian (2000), "From Nozick to Welfare Rights," *Critical Review*, Vol. 14, No. 4, pp. 481-501.

Barnett, Randy (1998), *The Structure of Liberty* (London: Oxford University Press).

Baudelaire, Charles (1957), *The Intimate Journals*, trans. Christopher Isherwood (Boston: Beacon Press).

Bell, Daniel (1996), *The Cultural Contradictions of Capitalism* (New York: Basic Books).

Bellah, Robert et al. (1985), *Habits of the Heart* (New York: Harper & Row Publishers),.

Brown, James Robert (1994), *Smoke and Mirrors, How Science Reflects Reality* (London: Routledge).

Capaldi, Nicholas (ed. 2005), *Business & Religion: A Clash of Civilizations* (M. & M. Scrivener Press).

Cowan, Tyler (2003), *Creative Destruction* (Princeton, NJ: Princeton University Press).

Den Uyl, Douglas J. (1991), *The Virtue of Prudence* (New York: Peter Lang).

Dennett, Daniel C. (1984), *Elbow Room, Varieties of Free Will Worth Having* (Cambridge, MA: MIT Press).

Deutsch, David (1997), *The Fabric of Reality* (London: Allen Lane).

Dworkin, Ronald (1978), *Taking Rights Seriously* (Cambridge, MA: Harvard University Press).

Dwyer, William (2001), "Do knowledge, ethics, and liberty require free will?" *The Journal of Ayn Rand Studies*, Vol. 3, No. 1, pp. 83-108.

Etzioni, Amitai (1993), *The Spirit of Community* (New York: Crown Publishing Co.).

Friedman, David (1973), *The Machinery of Freedom* (New York: Harper & Row).

Gilder, George (1981), *Wealth and Poverty* (New York : Basic Books).

Holmes, Stephen and Sunstein, Cass R. (1999), *The Cost of Rights: Why Liberty Depends on Taxes* (New York: W.W. Norton).

Hugo, Victor (1973), *La preface de Cromwell*, ed. Maurice A. Souriau (Geneve: Slatkine Reprints).

Kelley, David (1974), "The Necessity of Government," *The Freeman* 24 (April).

Kenny, Anthony (2004), *The Unknown God* (London & New York: Continuum).

Kincaid, Harold (1996), *Philosophical Foundations of the Social Sciences: Analyzing Controversies in Social Research* (London: Cambridge University Press).

Lapin, Rabbi Daniel (2004), "Judaism, Commerce, and Business," a paper given at "The Ethics of Commerce Conference," June 10-12, 2004, Loyola University, New Orleans, Louisiana.

Libet, B., Freeman, A. & Sutherland, K. (ed. 1999), *The Volitional Brain* (Exeter: Imprint Academic).

Long, Roderick T. & Machan, Tibor R. (ed. 2007), *Anarchy/Minarchy* (Burlinton, VT: Ashgate).

Machan, Tibor R. (1974), *The Pseudo-Science of B. F. Skinner* (New Rochelle, NY: Arlington House Publishing Co. Inc.).

Machan, Tibor R. (ed. 1974), *The Libertarian Alternative* (Chicago: Nelson-Hall).

Machan, Tibor R. (1975), *Human Rights and Human Liberties* (Chicago, IL: Nelson-Hall).

Machan, Tibor R. (1980) "Rational Choice and Public Affairs," *Theory and Decision 12* (September), pp. 229-58.

Machan, Tibor R. (1981) "Wronging Rights," *Policy Review 17* (Summer), pp. 37-58.

Machan, Tibor R. (1982), "Epistemology and Moral Knowledge," *The Review of Metaphysics,* Vol. 36, pp. 23-49.

Machan, Tibor R. (1989), *Individuals and Their Rights* (La Salle, IL: Open Court Publishing Co., Inc.).

Machan, Tibor R. (1990), *Capitalism and Individualism: Reframing the Argument for the Free Society* (New York: St. Martin's Press).

Machan, Tibor R. (1992), "Between Parents and Children," *Journal of Social Philosophy,* Vol. 23 (Winter), pp. 16-22.

Machan, Tibor R. (1998a), *Classical Individualism, The Supreme Importance of Each Human Being* (London: Routledge).

Machan, Tibor R. (1998b), "The Normative Basis of Economic Science," *Economic Affairs,* Vol. 18 (June), pp. 43-46.

Machan, Tibor R. (1998c), *Generosity; Virtue in Civil Society* (Washington, DC: Cato Institute).

Machan, Tibor R. (2000), *Initiative: Human Agency and Society* (Stanford, CA: Hoover Institution Press).

Machan, Tibor R. (ed. 2001), *Individual Rights Reconsidered* (Hoover Institution Press).

Machan, Tibor R. (2002), *The Right to Private Property* (Stanford, CA: Hoover Institution Press).

Machan, Tibor R. (2006), "Rand & Choice," in *The Journal of Ayn Rand Studies* Vol. 7, No. 2 (Spring), pp. 257-73.

Machan, Tibor R. (forthcoming), "Aristotle & the Moral Status of Business," *Journal of Value Inquiry* (forthcoming).

Machan, Tibor R. and Chesher, James E. (1999), *The Business of Commerce, Examining an Honorable Profession* (Stanford, CA: Hoover Institution Press).

Machan, Tibor R. and Chesher, James E. (2003), *A Primer on Business Ethics* (Lanham, MD: Rowman & Littlefield).

McKinnon, Catherine (1996), *Only Words* (Cambridge, MA: Harvard University Press).

Marx, Karl (1971), *Grundrisse*, trans. D. McLennan (New York: Harper Torch).

Marx, Karl (1977), "On The Jewish Question," in Karl Marx, *Selected Writings*, ed., D. McLellan (London: Oxford University Press).

Miller, Arthur (1995/1996), "In Memoriam," *The New Yorker*, December 25, 1995 & January 1, 1996.

Miller, Fred D. Jr. (1995), *Nature, Justice, and Rights in Aristotle's Politics* (Oxford: Clarendon Press).

Neuhaus, Richard John (1975), *Time Toward Home: The American Experiment in Revelation* (Seabury Press).

Nickel, James W. (1978–79), "Is There a Human Right to Employment?" *Philosophical Forum 10* (Winter-Summer), p. 164.

Norton, David L. (1976), *Personal Destinies, A Philosophy of Ethical Individualism* (Princeton, NJ: Princeton University Press).

Nozick, Robert. (1974), *Anarchy, State, and Utopia* (New York: Basic Books).

Nussbaum, Martha (1992), "Human Functioning and Social Justice: In Defense of Aristotelian Essentialism," *Political Theory*, Vol. 20, No. 2 (May), p. 231.

O'Connor, Timothy (2000), *Persons and Causes: The Metaphysics of Free Will* (New York: Oxford University Press).

Peden, Joseph R. (1977), "Property Rights in Celtic Irish Law," *Journal of Libertarian Studies*, 1 (Spring), pp. 81-95.

Pols, Edward (1982), *Acts of Our Being* (Boston, MA: University of Massachusetts Press).

Poole, Robert W. Jr. (1976), "Fighting Fires for Profit," *Reason*, May, pp. 6-11.

Rasmussen, Douglas B. and Den Uyl, Douglas J. (1990), *Liberty and Nature* (Chicago, IL: Open Court Publishing Co., Inc.).

Rand, Ayn (1964) *The Virtue of Selfishness* (New York: Signet).

Rand, Ayn (1973), "Government Financing in a Free Society," in E.S. Phelps, ed., *Economic Justice* (Baltimore: Penguin Books), pp. 363-67.

Rorty, Richard (1991), "The Seer of Prague", *The New Republic*, July 1, 1991, pp. 35–40.

Rosebaum, A. (ed. 1980), *The Philosophy of Human Rights* (Westport, CT: Greenwood Press).

Sadowsky, James (1974), "Private Property and Collective Ownership," in Machan (ed. 1974).

Shue, Henry (1970), *Basic Rights* (Princeton: Princeton University Press).

Skoble, Aeon (1992) "Another Caricature of Libertarianism," *Reason Papers*, No. 17, pp. 107-112.

Smith, Adam (1936), *The Wealth of Nations* (New York: Modern Library Edition).

Smith, Adam (1994), *The Wealth of Nations* (Indianapolis, IN: Liberty Classics).

Somerset Maugham, W. (1970), *A Writer's Notebook* (Westport, CT: Greenwood Press).

Sperry, Roger W. (1976), "Changing concepts of consciousness and free will," *Perspectives in Biology and Medicine*, Autumn, pp. 9-19.

Sperry, Roger W. (1983), *Science and Moral Priority* (Columbia University Press).

Spragens, Thomas A. (1982), *The Irony of Liberal Reason* (Chicago: University of Chicagor Press).

Sterba, James P. (1997), "Progress in Reconciliation: Evidence from the Right and the Left," *Journal of Social Philosophy*, Vol. 28 (Fall), p. 102.

Taylor, Charles (1985), *Philosophy and the Human Sciences* (London: Cambridge University Press).

Taylor, Charles (1989), *Sources of the Self: the Making of the Modern Identity* (Cambridge, MA: Harvard University Press).

Tolstoya, Tatyana (1992), "The Grand Inquisitor," *The New Republic*, June 29, 1992, p. 33.

Trucker, Robert C. (ed. 1978), *The Marx-Engels Reader* (New York: W.W. Norton).

Tuck, Richard (1977), "Is There a free-rider problem, and if so, what is it?" In *Rational Action*, ed. R. Harrison (Cambridge: Cambridge University Press, pp. 147-156).

Wills, Gary (2004), "The Bishops vs. the Bible," *The New York Times*, June 27, 2004, WK, p. 13.

Zeller, Eduard (1897), *Aristotle and the Earlier Peripatetics,* trans. B.F.C. Costelloe and J. H. Muirhead (London: Oxford University Press).

Zweig, Paul (1958), *The Heresy of Self Love* (second edition 1980).

Index

Jesus 117
Jordan, Michael 55

Kant, Immanuel 7n, 32, 79, 114n, 115, 116
Kelley, David 33, 61n
Keynes, John Maynard 30
Kincaid 65
Kirk, Russell 101n

Lapin, Daniel 109
liberalism 24
Libet, B. 10n
Limbaugh, Rush 112n
Lincoln, Abraham 38
Locke, John 37n, 69n, 75, 100, 103, 106
Lockean 20, 61, 105n, 106
Long, Roderick T. 23n

Mack, Eric 65n
MacKinnon, Katherine 53
Machan, Tibor 10n, 23n, 37n, 40n, 60, 61n, 67n, 68n, 69n, 82n, 88n, 102n, 104n, 105n, 108n, 113n, 114n, 115, 117n, 119n
Marx, Karl 24, 27, 34, 64n, 66, 69, 69n, 74, 76, 84
Marxism 4, 24, 72, 83
Maugham, W. Somerset 17
Meacham, Jon 14n
Mill, John Stuart 76
Miller, Arthur 109
Miller, Jr., Fred D. 65n, 68n
Mindszenty, Cardinal 22
minimum wage 98
miracles 15
Mozart, Wolfgang Amadeus 118

natural law 75
natural rights 100
naturalist 20
neo-Marxists 24
Neuhaus, Richard John 11, 16
Norton, David 65n, 110n, 115
Nozick, Robert 23, 102n
Nussbaum, Martha 111

objectivism 14, 23
Ockham, William of 69n
O'Connor, Timothy 9n
Orwell, George 21

Peden, Joseph 62n
Pierce, C. S. 13n
Plato 7n, 25, 26, 30
Pols, Edward 67n

Poole, Robert 59n
private property 48
public use 52
Porter, Cole 15

Rand, Ayn 9, 10, 24, 33, 61, 65n
Rasmussen, Douglas 65n, 82
Redford, Robert 55
Rembrandt 118
Rorty, Richard 28
Rousseau, Jean-Jaques 94

segregation 39
serfdom 90
Shue, Henry 101n, 102
Sinatra, Frank 98
Skoble, Aeon 105n
slavery 39, 53, 89, 92, 96
Smith, Adam 76, 86, 86n, 116
Socrates 25
Sperry, Roger W. 9, 118n
Spinoza 12, 16
Spragens, Thomas 24, 105n
Sterba, James 82, 101, 101n, 102n, 103
Stalinist 22
Sterner, Max 27, 33
Sunstein, Cass R. 101n, 102
surplus wealth 83

taxation 91, 93, 96
Taylor, Charles 24, 37, 74, 75n, 103n, 104, 105n
Thomist 12, 16, 114, 117
Thurmond, Strom 53
Tocqueville, Alec 87
Tolstoya, Tatiana 34
tragedy of commons 80
tribalism 73
Tuck, Richard 62
Turiano, Mark 13n

United Nations 94
Utopia 99
welfare state 34, 92, 94, 97, 99

Williams, Walter 112
Wills, Gary 117n
Wittgenstein 118
Wright, Frank Lloyd 118

Zeller, Eduard 68n
Zeno 108
Zweig, Paul 26

SOCIETAS: essays in political and cultural criticism

Public debate has been impoverished by two competing trends
On the one hand the trivialization of the media means that in-depth commentary has given way to the ten second soundbite. On the other hand the explosion of knowledge has increased specialization, and academic discourse is no longer comprehensible.

This was not always so — especially for political debate. But in recent years the tradition of the political pamphlet has declined. However the introduction of the digital press makes it possible to re-create a more exciting age of publishing. *Societas* authors are all experts in their own field, but the essays are for a general audience. The books are available retail at the price of £8.95/$17.90 each, or on bi-monthly subscription for only £5/$10. Details at **imprint-academic.com/societas**

IMPRINT ACADEMIC, PO Box 200, Exeter, EX5 5YX, UK
Tel: (0)1392 851550   Fax: (0)1392 851178   sandra@imprint.co.uk